Lotta Crabtree

Lotta Crabtree
Gold Rush Fairy Star

Lois V. Harris

PELICAN PUBLISHING COMPANY
GRETNA 2017

*The word "Pelican" and the depiction of a pelican are
trademarks of Pelican Publishing Company, Inc., and are
registered in the U.S. Patent and Trademark Office.*

Library of Congress Cataloging-in-Publication Data

Names: Harris, Lois V., author.
Title: Lotta Crabtree : gold rush Fairy Star / Lois V. Harris.
Description: Gretna : Pelican Publishing Company, [2017] | Includes
  bibliographical references and index.
Identifiers: LCCN 2016055908| ISBN 9781455622306 (hardcover : alk. paper) |
  ISBN 9781455622313 (e-book)
Subjects: LCSH: Crabtree, Lotta, 1847-1924—Juvenile literature. |
  Entertainers—United States—Biography—Juvenile literature.
Classification: LCC PN2287.C645 H37 2017 | DDC 792.4302/8092 [B] —dc23
LC record available at https://lccn.loc.gov/2016055908

Printed in Malaysia

Published by Pelican Publishing Company, Inc.
1000 Burmaster Street, Gretna, Louisiana 70053

In memory of my brother, John Bowers, a longtime San Franciscan

Contents

Preface and Acknowledgments

Years ago when I lived in San Francisco, I often passed a fountain on Market Street. I didn't know anything about it until recently when I visited the city. In the historic Palace Hotel, I joined a tour and saw a painting of famous San Franciscans by Antonio Sotomeyer. I learned that the redheaded figure in his picture was Lotta Crabtree. She had performed as a girl in the city during the Gold Rush and became a beloved national star. In 1875 she presented to San Francisco citizens the fancy fountain across the street from this hotel.

Curious about Lotta, I researched her inspiring life and decided to write her biography. I learned that hundreds gather at the fountain every year at dawn on April 18 for a ceremony. They sing songs as a band plays. At the moment the 1906 Earthquake struck, they bow their heads in silence.

Lotta Crabtree would be pleased that so many years after she gave her gift, the fountain continues to play a role in the city that held a special place in her heart. You can see Lotta's Fountain at the intersection of Market, Geary, and Kearny Streets in San Francisco.

Many thanks to Esther Noyes of the Anacortes Public Library, Anacortes, Washington; Karen Prasse with the Burlington Public Library, Burlington, Washington; and Robert Lopresti at Western Washington University Libraries, Bellingham, Washington. Their super-sleuthing skills helped me learn more about Lotta and obtain a copy of the play *Little Nell and the Marchioness*.

Lotta, by Chas. H. Crosby & Co., ca. 1870-1880
(Courtesy California History Room, California
State Library, Sacramento, California)

Introduction

In the 1800s, many American children worked to earn money for their poor families. Some entertained by acting, dancing, playing a musical instrument, or singing. At no other time in history did so many young performers appear in live theater events.

After gold was discovered in California in 1848, thousands of adventurers traveled there from around the world to dig for gold. Entertainers of all ages came to get rich, too, and toured the mining camps and towns. The miners rarely saw children, and they marveled at the ones who performed. They called them Fairy Stars, and one was their pet. Her name was Lotta Crabtree.

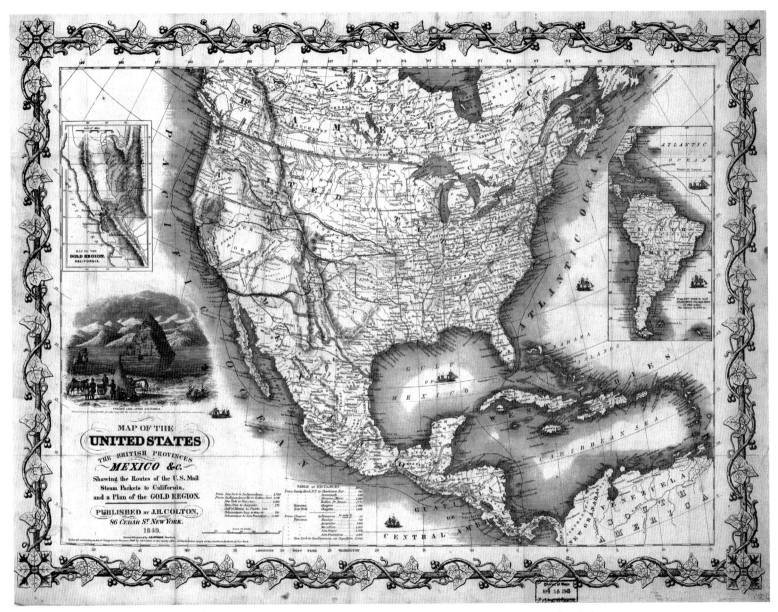

Map of the United States, the British provinces, Mexico &c., 1849, by John M. Atwood. Notice how far Lotta and her mother would have to travel from New York to get to the other side of the United States. (Collections of the Geography and Maps Division, Library of Congress)

Chapter 1

Ho! To California

Lotta peeked around the curtain. Candles flickered in bottles edging the stage, and tobacco smoke hung in the air. The rumble of miners' voices filled the log cabin. She hung back. She didn't want to perform for strangers! But her mama needed money. Her mother whispered a joke in her ear, and ten-year-old Lotta smiled. She felt her mama's firm hand on her back, pushing her forward.

With arms at her sides, Lotta stepped, hopped, skipped, and clicked her heels across the rough, wooden floor. Her red curls bounced, and her dark brown eyes sparkled as she danced jigs and reels and sang popular tunes. When she finished, the men applauded and whooped, tossing bills, coins, and golden nuggets at her feet.

She scooped the glittering lumps into her stovepipe hat. The top had a hole—her earnings fell out. She looked up with twinkling eyes as her mouth dropped open. The audience howled with laughter while her mother swept the gold and money into her satchel.

Lotta's earnings paid for her family's food and other household essentials. Her parents, Mary Ann and John Crabtree, had come from England to New York City. Her papa owned a bookstore, and her mama worked as a seamstress. Charlotte—or Lotta, as she was soon called—was born on November 7, 1847. Eleven weeks later and thousands of miles west, James Marshall discovered gold at Sutter's Fort in California. The news thrilled the world. Thousands of people left their families and work to strike it rich in the gold fields. Newspapers called these fortune hunters Argonauts after the gold seekers in ancient tales.

John caught gold fever and dreamed of going West. He often walked down to the harbor where hundreds of travelers boarded ships for California. When Lotta was four, he sold his bookstore, kissed her and Mary Ann goodbye, and set off. Lotta's mother told the relatives, "Nothing would do but Crabtree must leave N.Y. and dig gold." She always called her husband Crabtree.

A year later, Lotta's father wrote that they should meet him in San Francisco, California—but sent no money. There were three ways to travel from New York to Gold Country. Her mother chose the fastest, a journey of two months. But this way also cost the most: $500. She didn't have enough funds, so for weeks and weeks she saved money from her wages.

In the spring of 1853, five-year-old Lotta and her mama waved goodbye to family and friends from a ship's deck. The vessel pulled away from shore, and the wind filled the sails. Lotta might have heard one of the sailors singing out,

"Blow, ye breezes, blow! We're off to Californi-o!" as she watched New York City shrink and disappear. They sailed south on the Atlantic Ocean. Soon she would see her papa.

As Lotta's ship steamed south to tropical Panama, the temperature rose. The air in their cabin below deck grew hot and stuffy. Mary Ann and the other ladies waved their fans as they sat on the crowded deck, seeking a breeze. Two weeks after leaving New York, they landed in Panama.

The sun burned Lotta's arms as she passed a stinky swamp choked with tall grasses and buzzing insects. Ahead, a train's chimney spouted a cloud of black smoke, and a conductor waved at the travelers and called, "All aboard!" He helped Mary Ann and Lotta up the high steps. Soon the train chugged down the track, and black cinders flew through the open windows. Twenty-three miles later, they reached the end of the line at the Chagres River. Dark-skinned natives loaded newspapers, luggage, mail sacks, and supplies into wooden canoes as the adventurers stepped down into the boats.

Using paddles and poles, the natives steered the canoes on the winding river. Showers of warm rain soaked the passengers as colorful birds chirped, frogs croaked, and parrots squawked. Butterflies fluttered over flowers, alligators slipped into the muddy water, and monkeys swung through the tall trees. Deep in the rain forest, they stopped at a village for the night. Native children stared at Lotta's red curls as she passed by. In a thatched hut, Mary Ann checked for fleas, scorpions, and snakes before Lotta fell asleep on a blanket on the ground.

The next morning, a string of mules waited outside. They would carry the passengers for thirteen miles through the thickest part of the jungle. Someone lifted Lotta onto one of the pack animals, and it followed the others along

From the East Coast, one of the three most popular routes to California was by ship, sailing south on the Atlantic Ocean, around Cape Horn at the tip of South America, and north on the Pacific Ocean to San Francisco. The trip was about 17,000 miles and could last four to six months. People endured boredom, seasickness, and bugs or worms in their food. Sometimes ships sank after catching fire, hitting rocks, or meeting storms with high winds and rough seas. Depending on the type of cabin in the ship, the voyage cost from $300 to $400.

Wreck & Burning of the Steamer Independence on the Island of Margarita, February 16th, 1853; 150 Lives Lost / From the Sketch of Mr. Cross, Passenger, by Britton & Rey, 1853. The long journey around the tip of South America brought many dangers. (Library of Congress)

the narrow, twisting trail above steep ravines. She passed the graves of other travelers and swatted the buzzing mosquitoes. She didn't want to be bitten! Her mama said people had died in Panama from fever when insects that carried diseases bit them.

After days of riding, a breeze brushed Lotta's flushed cheeks. Through the rustling palm trees, she glimpsed white buildings and blue water. A cheer rose from the exhausted travelers. They had reached Panama City on the Pacific Ocean!

Another possibility was to travel overland by wagon train from Missouri to the Sierra Nevada Mountains in California. The journey of 2,000 miles cost about $600 for a family of four. During the three- to six-month trip across rugged land, pioneers might encounter unfriendly Indians, food and water shortages, high temperatures, early snows, and tornados.

The third and fastest way cost around $500 and took about two to three months. Travelers like Lotta and her mother sailed on the Atlantic Ocean to Panama in Central America, about 5,500 miles. Crossing the narrowest part of Panama could then take ten days. In the steamy jungle, some adventurers died from yellow fever, dysentery, or typhoid. Reaching the Pacific Ocean, another ship carried them north for about 3,400 miles to San Francisco.

Mountain Meadows from Nature, by S. H. Redmond, ca. 1877. Note the Indians hiding behind rocks. (Library of Congress)

Crossing the Isthmus, by Frank Marryat, 1855. Travelers from the United States were not accustomed to the climate of the Panamanian jungle and faced challenges going through it. (Courtesy California History Room, California State Library, Sacramento, California)

Since the discovery of gold in California, thousands of Argonauts had come to the port. New hotels, saloons, and gambling houses opened as the travelers sometimes waited weeks for passage on a ship to California.

Lotta and her mother soon boarded the SS *Oregon*. From the deck, they watched the green shore slip away as the ship steamed north on the Pacific Ocean. Mary Ann said they would see Lotta's papa in about two and a half weeks.

Flocks of birds floated on the waves, porpoises dove, and whales swam by. Now and then, Lotta spotted land or a distant passing ship. Many of the passengers spent the day on deck sharing amazing stories about folks easily discovering large nuggets of gold. But everyone was weary and eager for the journey to end. Then one day, a sailor finally yelled, "Land ho!"

Mary Ann and Lotta rushed to the deck's railing as passengers cried, "San Francisco, California!" The *Oregon* steamed into Golden Gate Harbor and steered around hundreds of empty ships swinging in the breeze. The captains and their crews had deserted their ships and fled to the mountains to dig for gold.

As sailors tied the *Oregon* to the dock with thick ropes, Lotta bounced from foot to foot. She leaned over the deck rail and looked down at the crowd. Where was Papa? She scampered ahead of her mama as they walked down the gangplank. People pushed and swirled around her. When her mother caught up, Lotta reached for her hand and held it tight.

Passengers cried happy tears, embraced their families, and left the wharf. Workers shouted and moved animals, cartons, crates, sacks, and fresh fruit from the ship. Horses, oxen, and mules pulling carts and wagons loaded with goods rolled away.

"Where is Papa?" Lotta wondered.

Mary Ann looked off into the distance and smiled. Old friends who had moved to San Francisco rushed over and greeted them. They said Crabtree was last seen panning for gold in the mountains. Tears filled Lotta's eyes. She hadn't seen her papa in almost two years. She and Mary Ann gathered their bags and followed their friends into the city.

Along the way, Lotta passed large ships resting on the street. One of their friends told her the abandoned ships had been pulled onshore and now were hotels or businesses. Then a man wearing a floppy hat, red flannel shirt, and pants stuffed into high leather boots strolled by. Lotta learned he was a miner like her father. Soldiers wearing guns and men with sparkling diamond pins in their shirts hurried by. Ladies rode in painted carriages pulled by high-stepping horses. Gold jewelry and pocket watches glowed in store windows.

Lotta's eyes danced at the sight of fancy candies displayed in one window. Through the shop's open door, she caught a whiff of something good. Someone was cooking chocolate, her mama said. Shacks and tents stood between the brick and wood buildings. As they climbed high up the sunny hill to their friends' home, away from San Francisco Bay, small houses and churches with steeples lined the streets.

Mary Ann rented a few rooms near Portsmouth Square, and they met their new neighbors. Some were entertainers, and the sounds of them singing or tinkling a piano drifted from their open windows. They had come to California to get rich, too, and said miners visit the city with gold in their pockets looking for a good time. People called San Francisco a good show town, but some performers toured in the mountains. Looking at Lotta, their neighbors told

Mary Ann that the gold diggers rarely saw children. And the prospectors paid good money to those who could entertain.

Later, Lotta and her mama went shopping in their new neighborhood. Lotta sniffed baking bread and roasting coffee. In a market, she tasted samples of figs, grapes, and pomegranates. They paused at a theater and gazed at the playbills announcing coming events. Lotta liked the pictures of entertainers and wanted to see a show. But Mama didn't buy tickets and told her she had to watch how much money she spent. Crabtree hadn't written, and she didn't know what she would do when her savings were gone. Lotta wished her papa would come to San Francisco. Didn't he want to see them? Didn't he care about them anymore?

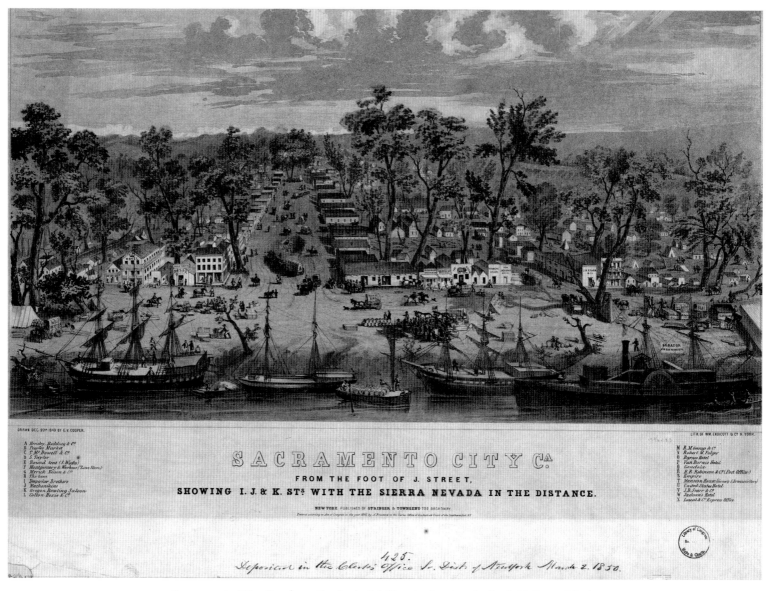

Sacramento City, Ca. from the foot of J. Street, showing I., J., & K. Sts. with the Sierra Nevada in the distance, by G. V. Cooper, 1849 (Library of Congress)

Chapter 2

Dancing and Singing Lessons

Six-year-old Lotta settled into her new life in San Francisco. One November day, the doors and windows in her house rattled, and the glasses on a shelf clinked. She noticed a picture on the wall had tilted. She and Mary Ann rushed outside to where their neighbors gathered. Their friends said an earthquake had occurred but told them not to be afraid, as this wasn't a big one.

Lotta listened to stories about stronger earthquakes when walls cracked, glass windows shattered, bricks tumbled from buildings, and waves raced across San Francisco Bay. She didn't feel the ground shaking where they were standing, and after a while, everyone returned to their houses. Lotta wondered if her papa had felt the earthquake up in the mountains, too.

Months passed, and still he had not come to San Francisco. Then he sent word for Lotta and her mother to join him in Grass Valley, a town east of San Francisco. After packing their clothes and saying goodbye to their friends, Lotta and Mary Ann hurried down to the harbor and boarded a steamboat. As bells rang, sailors shouted and untied lines. Several passengers cheered and cried, "Away to the Gold Fields!" Up the twisting Sacramento River they sailed.

Most of the passengers carried canvas sacks bulging with pickaxes, shovels, and pans. Some wore large wicker basket hats, and their long braids hung down their backs. Other travelers had on brightly colored serapes and sombreros. Lotta heard people speaking in English with foreign accents and in languages she couldn't understand. Men crowded the deck, and she saw only a few women and children.

The next day, the boat was tied up among dozens of ships lining the riverbank at Sacramento City. Lotta and Mary Ann walked up the road past tents. From a nearby shed, the sound of a blacksmith's hammering rang through the air. They came to a street of hotels and shops with wooden awnings shading a boardwalk. Miners loaded supplies onto wagons pulled by mules. Men on horseback rode by calling to their friends, and laughter spilled from a saloon's open door. Lotta glimpsed men inside gathered around a table playing cards.

Up the street, people boarded a large stagecoach. A driver stuffed canvas and leather bags, supplies, and bundled newspapers on top. Hitched to the coach were six horses. They snorted, shook their heads, and swished their tails. Lotta wished she could have a pony or a horse. Maybe someday. Mary Ann and Lotta handed their bags to the driver. He helped them inside the coach, and Lotta slipped in next to her mama on the leather seat.

Soon the driver called "G-long! H-up!" to his horses. With a jerk, they rocked and rolled out of town on a rough road. Mary Ann and the other travelers chatted. A dusty breeze blew through the open window. Lotta glimpsed white clouds in a bright blue sky floating above brown foothills. Soon she would see her papa.

In Grass Valley, Lotta and Mary Ann finally reunited with Crabtree. Everyone hugged and kissed and shared their news. Lotta learned her father had not found any gold, but he had an idea. He had rented a large house, and they would open a boarding house to make money. Prospectors paid in gold for their lodging and meals, and there was a shortage of places where they could stay in town. Papa said some miners were happy to sleep on a floor.

The Crabtrees moved into their new home, and in no time several miners boarded with them. Crabtree left every day to pan for gold and didn't help Lotta's mother much. In the kitchen, Lotta killed ants and chased lizards outside while Mary Ann grumbled. She wasn't used to cooking for so many people. The men told her groups of traveling entertainers including children sometimes came to town.

As in San Francisco, the ones who sang and danced were a wonder. Miners called them Fairy Stars, and the youngsters earned good wages. So Mary Ann signed Lotta up for dancing lessons.

Behind Lotta's home, birds sang in the pine trees, and rabbits, squirrels, and deer darted through the tall grass. Tucked in her bed at night, Lotta listened to coyotes bark, owls hoot, and rats race across the roof. Her parents warned her not to wander too far from the house and to keep an eye out for bears. She had spotted one—in a neighbor's yard.

The bear belonged to the actress Lola Montez, who kept it as a pet tied to a rope next to her home. Born in Ireland as Eliza Gilbert, Lola changed her name and pretended she came from Spain. Sometimes she spoke with an accent. Lola had toured across America and appeared in San Francisco

Grass Valley is about fifty miles north of Sacramento and not far from the American River, where in 1848 John Marshall discovered gold. It was a peaceful spot with grazing cows, log huts, and tents. But once the Argonauts came, within five years it boomed to a town of 3,500 with over 200 wooden buildings. Cabins, hotels, houses, saloons, a school, stores, and a theater edged the streets.

How to Pan for Gold

Put some dirt from a river or stream into a pan. Add water, swish, and let some dirt slop over the pan's rim. The glimmering gold is heavier than the dirt and settles to the bottom, making it easy to spot and remove.

California's gold diggers repeated this over and over until the sun set. Many times they stood in knee-deep icy mountain water. The men rarely discovered large nuggets. If the prospectors found an ounce of gold dust or flakes in a day, they were considered lucky. One ounce was worth between $8 and $16; the value changed daily. The miners used their gold as currency, and the banks, hotels, and shops had scales to weigh the gold. But the gold traders usually paid the miners about half of the gold's real value in coins.

LOLA MONTEZ AS MARIQUITA,
IN THE BALLET UN JOUR DE CARNEVAL OF SEVILLE.

Lola Montez as Mariquita in the ballet *Un jour de carneval of Seville*, by Nathaniel Courier, 1852. The star performs a Spanish dance. (Jerome Robbins Dance Division, New York Public Library for the Performing Arts, Astor, Lenox and Tilden Foundations)

in a play called *School for Scandal*, where she performed her famous Spider Dance. In a dress that barely covered her knees, she kicked high and shook her petticoats to get rid of imaginary spiders.

Over cups of tea, Grass Valley ladies gossiped about Lola. She smoked, had been married in Europe to a nobleman, and married again in San Francisco without getting divorced—*and* she showed her legs. In the 1850s, ladies hid their legs under long skirts. Mary Ann didn't care what others thought about Lola. She liked her. The performer was *famous*. She gave fancy parties and invited entertainers and the neighborhood children.

At her first party at Lola's house, Lotta studied the strangers and ate candy and iced cakes. She listened to songs and stories, played games, and giggled. Her tiny foot also tapped to the music that was playing. The star noticed her, and a few days later she invited Lotta to come for dance lessons. Lola taught her the Scottish Highland Fling and the Spanish Fandango, as well as how to sing popular tunes before an audience—and ride a horse. Lotta liked her new friend, and they rode around town and sometimes up into the rolling hills.

In the summer of 1854, Mary Ann had a baby boy. Lotta's parents named him John, after Lotta's father, and called him Jack for short. Seven-year-old Lotta helped care for her brother and continued taking lessons from Lola. But her father couldn't stop dreaming of finding gold. He heard of a place where he just knew he would strike it rich and declared they were moving.

Lotta didn't want to leave her friends, Lola, and their good times. But nevertheless, the Crabtrees soon left town. Their wagon clinked and clanged as they rode toward a distant line of snowy peaks. Crabtree said they were the

Sierra Nevada Mountains, and that's where they would live.

On the way, they passed green meadows sprinkled with yellow buttercups. Flocks of ducks rested on lakes, and geese honked as they flew overhead. Sometimes Lotta heard shouts and voices and peered down through the trees at miners in red shirts working by tumbling streams. The road climbed, and the air cooled in the green forest. The wagon turned into a wide clearing dotted with stumps and a few trees. Smoke curled from log cabins. Lotta had arrived in her new home: Rabbit Creek, California.

Years later, Lotta recalled those days. "I saw mining, life, the real thing. There the gold fever raged hot and I was in the midst of it. Of course, life was rough; but I want to tell you the miners were good fellows." She went on to describe the mining camp's saloon keeper, Mart Taylor, who also managed the theater. He "had eleven kinds of air castles, packed up in his carpet bag. They toppled over as soon as he set them up. . . . He had a knack of teaching. He got up an orchestra and led it and when he found that I had some talent in that line he offered to give me lessons."

Despite what he thought would be a sure thing, Lotta's father didn't find gold in Rabbit Creek. The sound of his axe splitting wood cut the chilly fall air. "We were very poor," Lotta remembered.

Mary Ann feared they would run out of money and opened another boarding house. Peddlers used mule trains to bring food, mail, and newspapers to the camp. They charged high prices for groceries. Vegetables were rarely

Right: *Miss Lotta, in her Irish Jig*, by H. W. Corbin, 1863 (Courtesy Special Collections, University of Nevada, Reno Libraries, UNRS-PO216)

MISS LOTTA,
IN HER IRISH JIG.
Published by H. W. CORBYN, San Francisco.

Gold Mining in California, by Currier & Ives, ca. 1871 (Library of Congress)

available. Some of the men who lived with the Crabtrees often shouldered their guns and vanished into the forest to hunt deer, elk, and quail. They brought back hunks of meat for Mary Ann to cook.

In the evenings after supper, Lotta listened to the men's stories about their adventures. One time they visited a village of wigwams in a nearby valley with trees of red and gold. The Native American chief and men made colorful feathered headdresses. The women carried babies on their backs and gathered acorns. They would grind the nuts to make bread and soup.

Mary Ann worried that she would not have enough food to feed the family and their boarders during the long winter. In their storeroom, she stowed boxes of salt and sacks of beans, coffee, flour, onions, and potatoes. Crabtree rolled in a barrel of butter and hung smoked hams from the ceiling. Lotta arranged cans of mackerel, cherries, peaches, and sardines on a shelf. She couldn't imagine they would eat all the food in that room!

Gray clouds now darkened the sky, and the wind blew. Days of steady rain turned the dusty road and forest trails to mud. Mule teams and wagons couldn't deliver fresh meat, goods, groceries, mail, and newspapers. The mining camp's link to the outside world disappeared.

Chapter 3

A Fairy Star

While fluffy snowflakes fell outside, Lotta stepped lightly and quickly in Mart Taylor's dance class next to his saloon. Sometimes he had to raise his voice to be heard over the laughing customers. He told Mary Ann her daughter was his best pupil and asked if Lotta could perform for the miners.

Lotta's mother thought it over. She needed money to buy food when the peddlers arrived in the mining camp in the spring. Some of their boarders owed her money, but she could not count on that. They promised to pay her when they found gold—if they were lucky. Mary Ann agreed to let Lotta perform and made her practice on their broad hearthstone. She told Lotta entertaining the miners would be fun, like a game.

Mart cobbled a pair of leather dancing shoes, and Mary Ann created a costume using scraps of material from old clothes. Her fingers flew as she sewed a pair of britches, a green coat, and a stovepipe hat. Lotta tried them on and twirled around the room while her mother laughed and said she looked like a leprechaun.

The days eventually warmed. As sunshine melted the snow, Mart spread the word around town about Lotta's first public performance. Before her debut, eight-year-old

Lotta pushed aside the curtain in the log cabin theater and peered at the crowd. She knew everyone there. Candles flickered at the edge of the stage, and tobacco smoke hung in the air. She took a breath and stepped out.

Lotta's lips curved in a smile, and she danced, giggled, and sang songs. The men cheered and clapped. "When I was through they roared applause, so much that I was terrified," she recalled, "and they threw to me nuggets of gold." Mary Ann swooped down and collected all of the gold in her apron.

Soon after this first performance, Lotta's father took his clothes, pan, pick, and shovel and left without writing a note. When Lotta asked where he had gone, her mama said Crabtree was off digging for gold somewhere. Days passed, and Lotta worried when he didn't return.

Mary Ann was weary from cooking and cleaning the boarding house, but she needed money. She and Mart decided to form a troupe that would tour the mining country, just like the entertainers who came to their town. Mary Ann had been practicing and could sing a little, shake a tambourine, and play a triangle. Mart would dance, strum his guitar, and write songs. Lotta would dance and sing and be the star of their show.

Lotta packed her bag and slipped her leprechaun costume in with her clothes. She did *not* want to perform for strangers, but her mama needed help. She hoped her papa would hurry home. Didn't he want to be with them anymore? Didn't he miss them?

In no time at all, Mart led them away from Rabbit Creek and on to a narrow forest trail. They all rode mules, and Mary Ann carried Jack. "We used to put up in little camps," Lotta remembered, "where we gave performances in a tent or a cabin." She danced on barrel tops, pool tables, or rough plank floors. Sometimes Mart built a platform for her by nailing boards to supports. He also made a curtain by rigging a rope across the room and hanging blankets on it.

Through the spring and summer, they traveled to mining camps and towns. But when they reached Northern California, Lotta learned that her mother could not go on; she was going to have another baby. Mary Ann sent Jack with Mart to San Francisco, a journey of two hundred miles. The toddler would stay with Lotta's aunt, who had recently moved there.

Mary Ann made arrangements with a pioneer family in Eureka, a city on the Pacific Ocean, to care for Lotta. She told Lotta she must stay with them for a while, and she would come for her in a few weeks. Lotta cried and pleaded. She didn't want to leave her mother and live with people she didn't know.

When a stranger arrived with two horses, Lotta clung to her mother before finally kissing her goodbye. The man helped her climb on the back of a horse and led her into the damp, dark forest. On the trail, large trees surrounded them, and green ferns, brown needles, and cones carpeted the ground.

Now and then, a shaft of sunlight pierced the dim light.

LOTTA.

87 UNION SQR., N. Y.

Lotta, photograph by Napoleon Sarony, 1871-1896 (Macauley's Theatre Collection, 1980.20.0307, Archives and Special Collections, Ekstrom Library, University of Louisville, http://digital.library.louisville.edu/cdm/ref/collection/macauley/id/314)

Lotta, who was now nine years old, patted her horse's soft hair as he jogged along. Looking up, she caught her breath. High above stretched the straightest, tallest trees she'd ever seen. Her guide said they were redwood trees, and more than 900 years old. Lotta had never heard of anything that old! She wished her mama could see them. A thickening fog wrapped around them, and Lotta wondered when she would see her. Her eyes filled with tears.

Miles later, the fog thinned and they rode out of the trees. The horses broke into a trot on a road that wound along a bay and into Eureka, a city of churches, homes, and shops. Lotta smelled something sweet in the air as they passed a large building. Her guide said it was a mill where they sawed redwood logs into lumber. Before long, he called out "whoa there" and pulled up on his horse's reins

in front of a large house. He lifted Lotta down from the horse as the front door opened.

The Ryan family welcomed Lotta, and in no time she was playing games with their children. Years later, they remembered when she danced and sang songs for them and made them laugh. In one tune, Lotta mimicked the way someone from England talked. She changed the sound of the lyrics and twanged, "I've a *howl* in my heart big enough to roll a cabbage around in."

After a few weeks, Mary Ann arrived with Lotta's new brother, George. Lotta hugged her mother long and tight and held the baby. When Lotta's mama said her papa would meet them in San Francisco, Lotta couldn't stop smiling. Mary Ann told her that potholes, ruts, and mud marked the roads through the forest to the city, so she had booked passage for them on a ship. They said goodbye to the Ryans and sailed south on the Pacific Ocean. Lotta helped her mama care for the baby during the voyage. Two days later, they landed in San Francisco.

"Eureka" is a Greek word that means "I found it!" In 1848, about the same time gold was found in the Sierra Nevada foothills, Maj. Pierson B. Reading discovered gold in the Trinity River in Northern California. Argonauts poured into the area. Settlers named their village on the Pacific Ocean Eureka. By 1855, ships from San Francisco steamed into the city's harbor and unloaded adventurers seeking gold. Workers loaded the vessels with lumber from Eureka's seven sawmills. The ships sailed to cities up and down the Pacific Coast. Carpenters and builders preferred the beautiful redwood because it resisted decay and insects.

"Eureka" is also California's motto and appears on the state seal. The word captures the spirit of the gold rush adventurers.

San Francisco's population soared from 500 in 1847, when gold was discovered at Sutter's Fort, to more than 55,000 in 1856. Gold seekers had come from around the world. Most of the adventurers traveled into the mountains, but others stayed and got rich by supplying people with whatever they needed. Luxury hotels, restaurants serving fancy food, shops offering the finest goods, and many theaters sprang up. Miners returned to the city looking for a good time with pockets bulging with gold. They risked losing their new fortune to criminals, gamblers, saloonkeepers, and Chinese opium peddlers.

Three years had passed since Lotta and her mother had lived in San Francisco. Now Lotta had two brothers and her father had returned—again, without any gold. The Crabtrees moved into a house, but Lotta didn't stay too long. Her mother needed money to feed and care for the family, so Lotta and Mary Ann left Crabtree, Jack, and George and joined Mart and a large troupe in the mountains.

After their shows, the entertainers traveled at night on dusty or muddy trails through forests and across rivers and valleys. Lotta was tired during these nighttime journeys, so they tied her to the back of a horse or mule, and someone grabbed the halter and rode ahead of her. Lotta slept as the animal jogged along. Coyotes barked and wolves howled. Stories of grizzly bears, robbers looking for gold or money, and horses and mules plunging down the sides of mountains made the performers fearful, so they were particularly careful and kept a close eye on their surroundings.

As the sun rose in the sky, the troupe would rest before their next event. Mary Ann and the others coached Lotta, and her performance skills improved. Jake Wallace, a musician, gave Lotta banjo lessons, and she strummed the instrument as she sang.

Lotta was one of the first female banjo pickers on the stage. Men said that the banjo was not an instrument for women. In fact, at that time, banjos were usually played by African American men. In Shasta, California, Lotta's troupe met a popular minstrel touring group from San Francisco. The white men blackened their faces and during their act pretended they were African Americans. Mary Ann knew one of the members of the troupe and asked if Lotta could perform by singing "Little Topsy's Song." Topsy is the unruly slave character in the play *Uncle Tom's Cabin*.

Lotta smeared a piece of burned cork over her skin to

Swell Negro Banjo Player, circa 1875, by Courier Co. (Library of Congress)

perform in blackface. An African American in her troupe had taught her to shuffle and tap in a soft-shoe dance. Lotta performed the dance with an easy grace and sang "Little Topsy's Song":

I can play the banjo, yes, indeed I can!
I can play a tune upon the frying pan,
I hollo like a steamboat 'before she's gwine to stop,
I can sweep a chimney and sing out at the top.

African Americans and white men in blackface performed in minstrel troupes in the United States from the 1840s until the early 1900s. White audiences enjoyed the shows and thought the humor reflected black culture. African Americans didn't think it was funny. The entertainers sang African American songs and exaggerated the way they talked, trying to sound like they were plantation slaves. The performers joked, acted in skits, and played banjos, fiddles, tambourines, and spoons. Minstrelsy, or minstrel shows, died out in the 1930s when African Americans played a new, lively music called jazz, which became popular around the world.

The play *Uncle Tom's Cabin* was based on a book with the same title that was read by millions of Americans. Written by Harriet Beecher Stowe, the 1852 novel tells the tale of a cruel slave owner, runaway slaves, and the effect of slavery on families. The book roused many Americans to try to end slavery and angered others who believed in the right to own slaves. Many songs inspired by the book and its characters were written after it was published.

Lotta Crabtree, by Mora, date unknown (Buffalo Bill Center of the West, Cody, Wyoming, P.71.201)

The miners applauded, and Lotta took several encores, "each time filling her slipper with money which was being showered on the stage."

Lotta's troupe continued on their tour of Northern California, and she kept adding more to her regular act. An actor showed her how to mime, or use gestures but no words. She rolled her eyes, twisted her face, and winked when she told jokes, too. When she tried her new skills onstage, the miners laughed. She giggled, and they whooped. Until then, only men performed comedy. Actresses didn't want to risk their ladylike reputations. Nine-year-old Lotta became the first female comedian.

Before every show, Lotta poked her curly red head out from behind the curtain and grinned at the audience, who responded with laughter and cheers. Little Lotta had them in the palm of her hand. Towards the end of the show, she changed from her leprechaun costume into a pretty dress with puffy sleeves and sang songs like "Dear Mother, I'll Come Home Again." Tears filled the homesick men's eyes. They cheered and applauded, usually tossing money and gold around her tiny feet. But if the miners were down on their luck, or if another group entertained nearby, Lotta's troupe earned little.

Chapter 4

The Early Years

Winter's rainy season turned the mountain roads to mud, and Lotta's tour ended. She and her mother returned to their San Francisco home. The city had prospered from the gold spent there by prospectors. Some bought real estate or started businesses.

By 1857, the Gold Rush was over. Miners with a pan and a mule could no longer make easy gold discoveries. Teams of men with heavy machinery went after the remaining ore in rocky and rugged places. Disappointed gold diggers farmed, found jobs, returned to their homes and families, or sailed across the Pacific Ocean to new gold fields in Australia. Most described their difficulties and troubles trying to strike it rich by using the popular expression "seeing the elephant."

On sunny days, Lotta and her mother strolled the streets past houses and restaurants with doors or windows flung open. At times, the breeze carried the scent of simmering apples and cinnamon, frying bacon and onions, or something mysterious simmering on a stove.

Many theaters dotted the city, and Lotta liked to read

San Francisco, by Frank Marryat, ca. 1850. The city of San Francisco flourished thanks to the Gold Rush. (Library of Congress)

the playbills. She studied the pictures of actors, actresses, circus people, dancers, magicians, musicians, and singers. Mary Ann said the famous performers appeared at the Opera House. Lotta dreamed of performing there, too, and asked if she could audition.

Lotta's father asked the owner, Tom Maguire, if Lotta could try out. The man refused. Crabtree boasted that the miners called his daughter their pet and a Fairy Star, but this did not convince Mr. Maguire. He said Lotta might be doing well performing for miners, but she wasn't good enough for his grand theater. When ten-year-old Lotta heard the news, she vowed that someday she would appear in Maguire's theater.

Mary Ann bustled about to find places where Lotta could perform and earn some money. Soon Lotta danced and sang in an auction house where clerks sold furniture and Chinese silk shawls. She performed in saloons and gambling houses—where proper ladies wouldn't dream of going. In these places, miners drank liquor to celebrate gold discoveries, forget their failures, or relieve loneliness. When Lotta finished her act, Mary Ann whisked her out the door quick as a wink.

Lotta moved on to melodeon theaters, which were venues popular only with men. They liked the lively, relaxed atmosphere, and tickets cost just twenty-five cents. The small theaters trained people for show business. Performers had to act, dance, sing, and play a musical instrument. Lotta mastered the hornpipe and drum and learned more dance steps. She could polka, shuffle, do an Irish jig, and dance a Scottish fling with high kicks. When the audience applauded, Lotta's feet flew faster. After the shows, her mama hurried her home.

Lotta had little free time for making friends or playing. She went to school sporadically; the longest stretch of time she attended was six months. Voice lessons, practicing, and rehearsals filled her days, and she performed most evenings. The money and gold she earned supported her family of five. Crabtree, who wore a beaver hat, cloak, and

Maguire's Opera House (Courtesy Collection of the Museum of Performance + Design, San Francisco, California)

polished boots, kept house and received an allowance. Mary Ann handled business and controlled the money. She rustled about in silk dresses, her faded red curls almost hidden by a bonnet that hugged her stern face.

Two years passed. When Lotta was twelve, she finally auditioned at the Opera House and won a boy's part in a play. At that time, most actresses turned down male roles. They wouldn't wear men's clothes, as people might think they weren't ladies. But Lotta liked dancing in britches. For one thing, they allowed her to kick high! She stuffed her hands in her pockets and strutted around. Her mother, on the other hand, said she looked tough and told Lotta she wanted her to act like a lady. Onstage one night, Lotta discovered that her mother had sewn up the pockets in her pants. She burst into tears and dashed into the wings. Her mother snipped the stitches. Sniffling, Lotta returned to the stage and finished her performance. Never again did Mary Ann tell her daughter what to do on the stage.

Sometimes Lotta performed in plays with other child stars, like the Worrell sisters. She fretted about Sophie, Irene, and Jennie's dancing. The sturdy sisters pounded and thumped their shoes on the wooden stage. But Lotta knew when to prance with delicate quick steps or hammer her heel or toe, or both. If the Worrells received longer or louder applause, Lotta sobbed in her dressing room. Yet people called her "Miss Lotta, the San Francisco Favorite."

Lotta made friends with the rest of the cast at the Opera House but wasn't allowed to attend their parties after the shows. Mary Ann shadowed her and brought her home each evening. Lotta's busy life kept her from having boyfriends, too.

The actor J. H. P. Gedge lived near Lotta's house when he was a teenager. He recalled picking "the prettiest rose in the neighborhood every day. I'd wrap it up carefully and throw it into her back yard after dark, for if her mother saw the act, woe to me!" The following day, he would see Lotta and her mother walking to the theater. "Always I managed to pass them somewhere when she would fondle the flower in recognition," he said, "and all this time we talked only with our eyes." Mary Ann never let Lotta stop and talk, hustling her on.

In 1861, shocking news rocked San Francisco— Southerners had fired on the Union Army in Fort Sumter,

Lotta Crabtree in britches smoking a cigar, photograph by J. Gurney & Son, circa 1868 (Library of Congress)

The Worrell Sisters, date unknown (Billy Rose Theatre Division, New York Public Library for the Performing Arts, Astor, Lenox and Tilden Foundations)

South Carolina. War had started between the North and the South! In the South, the Civil War was called the War of Southern Independence. Northerners looked at it differently and said it was the War of Rebellion.

Most residents in San Francisco sided with Northerners and wanted the Union soldiers to win the war. Performers pleased their audiences by singing or playing lively songs showing their loyalty to the North. Mary Ann sewed a blue soldier's uniform like the Union Army's. Lotta, age fourteen, wore the costume during a new act in which she played a

Lotta, photograph by Napoleon Sarony, 1871-1896. Lotta in her Union Army costume. (Macauley's Theatre Collection, 1980.20.0304, Archives and Special Collections, Ekstrom Library, University of Louisville, http://digital.library.louisville.edu/cdm/ref/collection/macauley/id/311)

drum and a hornpipe and sang songs praising the nation. People leaped from their theater seats and marched in the aisles to her music!

At about the same time, talk of new gold and silver discoveries electrified the city. Miners in California's camps rushed east on rugged mountain trails to Nevada Territory. Lotta and her mama waved goodbye to her brothers and Crabtree; they piled into a stagecoach with five other musicians and singers, and the troupe followed the fortune hunters to Virginia City, Nevada.

As the crowded stagecoach bounced along, Lotta enjoyed the entertainers' jokes and stories. She had worked with all the men. Jake Wallace, her banjo teacher, managed the troupe and drove their stagecoach. He remembered one incident after heavy rains flooded the rivers and streams. At the raging American River, the horses galloped across a bridge. With a loud thud, the bridge shook. Jake heard

grinding and held the reins tight. Lotta stuck her head out the window and shouted over the roaring water, "Stay with 'em, Jake! Stay with 'em!" The horses reached the road, and everyone looked back and gasped. The bridge had turned over and tumbled downstream.

The company continued on into the forests of Northern California. During their shows, folks shouted approval and applauded after Jake sang a tune about the United States. When Lotta performed her act in her blue Union soldier costume, audiences stood and cheered.

The troupe rolled on through timberland and into southern Oregon and opened their show in a theater in Roseburg. After each patriotic song, the crowd mumbled, snickered, and snorted, growing louder every time. The miners were from the South.

Lotta was not intimidated. She thrummed her drum and began. Her clear voice carried to the back of the theater

---

For years, Northerners and Southerners held different opinions about taxes. They also disagreed about whether the federal government had the right to make rules about slavery or even abolish it within the states. By 1861, several Southern states had left the Union. They believed they had a right to own slaves. The Southerners elected a president, formed a Confederate Army, and prepared to go to war.

Northerners wanted to do away with slavery and stood with the Union Army. Pres. Abraham Lincoln hoped for a compromise and wished to avoid war. People across the country expressed strong opinions about which side to support.

Brass bands played the popular Northern tune "Rally Round the Flag." Union soldiers on the battlefield, in the trenches, and on the march sang the lyrics.

Southern soldiers had a good song, too. In 1861, Harry Macarthy wrote "The Bonnie Blue Flag." It became a rallying song for soldiers and supporters of the Confederacy.

Hurrah! Hurrah! For Southern rights; hurrah!
Hurrah! for the Bonnie Blue Flag has gain'd th'
Eleventh star.

Publishers in the North and South rushed to print thousands of copies of each song for cards, sheet music, and songbooks.

over rising hisses and hoots as she sang the rousing song "Rally Round the Flag." It was also called "The Battle Cry of Freedom" and was written by George F. Root in 1862. The chorus follows:

> The Union forever! Hurrah, boys, hurrah!
> Down with the traitor, up with the star,
> While we rally round the flag, boys, rally once again,
> Shouting the battle cry of freedom.

Jake called to Lotta to change her costume and cancel the soldier act—they could be mobbed! She raised her chin and said she was for the North and "would give it [even] if they hanged her that night."

Fifteen-year-old Lotta continued performing. Jake said, "She faced a cold and relentless audience and they never gave her a hand." When she finished, no shower of gold and money fell on the stage. The curtain dropped, and the cast dashed out the door, jumped into their waiting stagecoach, and raced out of Roseburg. "She was a little mite of a thing," said Jake, "but she had sand and ginger in her enough for a dozen people."

Chapter 5

Miss Lotty

Soon after Lotta returned to San Francisco following this tour, a group of volunteer firemen asked her to give a benefit concert. She had waited two years for this invitation! Performers considered it an honor to give a benefit performance. Even visiting actors and actresses were expected to give at least one. Firemen bought most of the concert tickets and marched to the theater as a brass band played. The events were splendid.

For the show, fifteen-year-old Lotta was billed as "Miss Lotty" and performed with other actors and actresses.

> Eighteen fire companies served San Francisco in the 1860s. More than 700 residents worked without pay as volunteer firemen. Wearing red shirts and fire hats, they hurried to blazes, dragging their engines. The firefighters included leading citizens, bankers, lawyers, wealthy merchants, and performers. Theater owners counted on a rapid response from the firemen to protect their property and the public. And fire departments depended on entertainers to raise money at benefits to buy equipment like buckets, hoses, carts, and pumper engines.

When it came time for her act, Lotta burst onto the stage dressed in her blue Union Army costume. As she sang "Rally Round the Flag," the cheering audience rose to its feet. Never still for a second, her head bobbed with the beat of the music as she blew a hornpipe. She scampered and danced, and the crowd applauded long and loud.

Now a favorite of the firemen, Miss Lotty gave one benefit after another in San Francisco. She also appeared with other performers in the Exhibition Hall at the Willows, a new amusement park. Posters described the entertainment as elegant.

Tickets to the Willows cost twenty-five cents. Located on

> In the 1860s, amusement parks popped up across the country. San Franciscans could spend the day at three popular parks with different attractions. They enjoyed shows, drank beer with friends in a garden, shot clay targets, or climbed into a wicker basket under a large hot air balloon and soared above the crowds. Listening to a tinkling piano, couples circled a dance floor. Men attended horse races while ladies admired a walk made of shells.

the edge of the city, a stream lined with willow trees and grass created a peaceful setting in the park. Lotta, who was now sixteen, sniffed the flowers, enjoyed the aquarium and museum, and gasped as stuntmen did daring tricks, resisting death.

After her show each afternoon, Lotta slipped on a dress with a hoop skirt that revealed her slim ankles. She and her mama rushed to catch a train. It steamed through the darkening farmland and into the cool, wispy fog of the city, where she often gave an evening performance at a theater.

One evening when Lotta was home, a young man came to her house. He wanted to take her for a ride in his horse and carriage. Lotta's mother said no and sent him away. For the next several days, Lotta swept the front porch after dinner, hoping he would come back. He never did.

A few days before Christmas in 1863, Lotta learned that her papa had been in a fight in front of the Opera House while a performance was going on inside. Firemen emptied the crowded theater. Sacramento and San Francisco papers printed the story. One reporter said, "John A. Crabtree, father of the melodeon actress known as Little Lotta, was talking with Tom Maguire. Crabtree drew a derringer [a small gun] and fired. Maguire struck down the weapon and

Portrait of a Young Girl, a 1900s reproduction of a photograph of Lotta from about the 1850s. She would wear dresses like this when she was not performing. (Courtesy California History Room, California State Library, Sacramento, California)

During the Gold Rush, half of San Francisco's residents owned guns. Violence occurred every day. Disputes sometimes led to fistfights, gunfights, and killings. People with criminal records mingled with the gold seekers. Thieves, robbers, and killers knew the Army couldn't control crime. Miners carried revolvers and hunting knives to protect themselves and their property.

the ball tore off a portion of Maguire's pantaloons. Crabtree was immediately arrested."

Another newspaperman wrote, "Crabtree was evidently in liquor at the time, and had been excited by the report that Maguire had made some remarks concerning his family or himself."

Lotta wished Crabtree didn't drink. Now many people knew he did. How would Tom Maguire treat her after this? Maybe she would never perform in the Opera House again.

About then, Tom Maguire hired Adah Menken, an actress who was on tour across America. Rumors swirled that he paid Adah $500 a performance. She enjoyed shocking audiences by revealing her flesh-colored tights when she rode her horse up a steep ramp onstage.

Adah attended one of Lotta's performances and met Lotta. The two young entertainers became friends. Besides being an actress, Adah was a published poet. San Franciscans spotted her in cafes dressed in yellow silk smoking thin black cigars with her many boyfriends. Mary Ann ignored the gossip about Adah being wicked. She liked the star; Adah was *famous*.

Lotta and Adah rode horses from the city to the Cliff House, a resort overlooking the Pacific Ocean. They laughed at the sea lions sunning themselves on the rocks. At a nearby racetrack, the two entertainers joined the crowd and leaped out of their seats, cheering for their favorite horses. Adah also told stories about the performers she had worked with and her experiences while touring. Lotta daydreamed that someday she would star in leading roles across America, too.

A critic had recently called Lotta "the most talented juvenile actress California has yet produced." But she longed for much more. She wanted to be a national favorite. For months, Lotta couldn't make up her mind: should she

Adah Isaacs Menken in her Extraordinary Equestrian Act, by R. J. Hamilton, Butler Collection of Theatrical Illustrations, Butler 346. Adah would often perform with a horse. (Manuscripts, Archives, and Special Collections, Washington State University Libraries)

stay in California, or should she try performing back East? She had made enough money to lead a comfortable life by performing on local stages, and the Civil War still raged. But her mama and Adah kept urging her to try New York City, the entertainment capital of America.

Finally, Lotta agreed. She gave her last performance at Tom Maguire's packed Opera House and earned $1,500 that evening. In the spring of 1864, she and her parents boarded the *St. Louis* and waved goodbye to her brothers and aunt. The ship steamed across the harbor and turned south, and the golden hills of the city Lotta called home disappeared. About a week later, the Crabtrees landed in Panama.

Lotta remembered when she was five and crossed the

California Scenery, Seal Rocks—Point Lobos, by Currier & Ives, 1863-1883. This painting shows the Cliff House, where Lotta and Adah would go to have fun. (Courtesy California History Room, California State Library, Sacramento, California)

tropical country by train, canoe, and mule. The journey took a week and a half. But this time it lasted only three hours, and she rode in a comfortable passenger railroad car. Her first-class ticket cost $25 for the forty-seven-mile trip from Panama City on the Pacific Ocean to Monkey Hill on the Atlantic Ocean.

From Panama, the Crabtrees continued north by ship on the Atlantic Ocean to New York. In May, Lotta arrived in the city where she was born. Mary Ann eagerly rented Niblo's Saloon, a popular theater. She hired a stage manager and a small company of actors, actresses, and comedians. She placed notices about the show in newspapers and had posters hung around the city proclaiming Lotta as "The California Favorite."

While Lotta rehearsed with the other performers, her father would disappear for hours at a time. When he returned, Lotta smelled whiskey on his breath.

Gold seekers crossing the jungle in Panama demanded a quicker and safer way to travel. In 1850, construction of a single track began not far from the Atlantic Ocean through swampland to the Chagres River. Work gangs built an iron bridge to carry railroad cars to the other side of the water. Across the river, the men persisted and continued cutting through jungle. Thousands died from accidents, malaria, and other diseases. The Panama Railroad cost $6,000,000 to build. In 1855, the first train packed with freight and passengers steamed from the Atlantic to the Pacific. By 1868, the railroad had safely carried millions of dollars in gold from California to ships on the Atlantic Ocean bound for Africa, Europe, and North and South America.

The show opened on Wednesday, June 1, 1864. That night in her dressing room, Lotta brushed black mascara on her eyelashes. She stared at herself in the mirror. Suppose she failed? California newspapers would print the news. Everyone would know. Her mama reminded her of past successes, fussed with Lotta's curls, and told jokes. A knock sounded at the door, and a voice called, "It's time!" Lotta followed Mary Ann to the wings.

Lotta slipped from behind the curtain and observed her first New York audience. The gaslights hissed. She moved forward and smiled. She danced, gave a banjo solo, sang, and appeared in a short comic play. The small crowd laughed and clapped. Lotta gave an encore and danced an Irish jig. But when the curtain dropped, her mouth drooped. In San Francisco, she played in theaters with few empty seats. Why hadn't more people come?

For the next night's show, Mary Ann tried to fill the theater by passing out many free tickets. The folks who received them showed their appreciation by loudly applauding and stomping their feet every time Lotta did something. Paying ticket holders stared at these silly people.

A newspaper theater critic who reviewed the show noted that an actor kept smoothing the ends of his moustache and the wrong scenes were brought onstage and pulled back. Instead of a kitchen setting, bedroom scenery was set up.

In one of Lotta's scenes, a stagehand wheeled on a wooden wall for the next performer's act. The critic

In the middle of the 1800s, some entertainers performed their routines in large buildings called concert halls rather than proper theaters. The performers sang, danced, played music, and did comedy skits in separate acts. Wage earners and laborers could afford the cheap tickets and enjoyed the variety of entertainment.

continued, "Lotta was heard all over the house crying, 'Change the scene,' and was obliged to walk off the stage."

The critic added, she "gives an Irish jig as well as we have ever seen it done . . . looks charming on the stage . . . and knows exactly how to put an audience in good humor." But "her style is certainly not intended for a first-class audience, concert halls being her proper stamping-ground."

For five more nights, Lotta endured. She performed before more and more empty seats. A sprinkling of applause followed her routines. As the curtain fell on the last night, she fled to her dressing room and bawled. Streaks of black mascara marked her cheeks. She had flopped in her New York debut.

Mary Ann paid the other entertainers, and Lotta and her parents boarded a train for the Midwest. Her mother had arranged for her to appear in a new show in Chicago, Illinois.

But as Lotta rehearsed for her upcoming performance, she kept thinking of the New York show. Suppose she failed again? What would she do?

Chapter 6

Something New and Daring

In Chicago, Lotta took several parts in a play. For one role, she dressed in a fairy costume and danced with delicate steps. In another, she acted as a bold, lively, likeable, ragged orphan who succeeds in the end. She loved playing this tomboy character and would do it for the rest of her career.

After the final curtain dropped one evening, Lotta stepped forward on the stage, smiling and bowing while the audience applauded. Admirers tossed bouquets of flowers at her feet, and one gentleman tied up a gold watch in handkerchiefs and threw the bundle onstage. The popular show ran for three weeks.

Mary Ann put Lotta's brothers, George and Jack, in a boarding school and paid the fees with her daughter's earnings. Lotta and her parents toured the Midwest, and when the Civil War ended in 1865, she also performed in the South. Americans wanted to forget the bad times and filled theaters looking for entertainment. Lotta learned to handle all kinds of audiences. A critic described the spectators as "delighted with the original acting, sweet singing, incomparable dancing and the great banjo solo." Another reporter said Lotta was "earning both fame and fortune."

A NIGHTMARE IN THE SLEEPING CAR.
"Oh, I was s-o-o dry!" Chorus,-"Dry up and bust."

A nightmare in the sleeping car: "oh, I was s-0-0 dry!" chorus,—"dry up and bust," by Currier & Ives, circa 1875. A thirsty passenger calls the porter to fill her glass of water and disturbs the sleep of the other travelers. (Library of Congress)

Lotta traveled by railroad and many times had to change trains again and again before she reached the location of her next performance. She slept in sleeping cars, cheap hotels, and boarding houses and grabbed a sandwich in railroad stations or ate in eating houses by the tracks.

In small towns and large cities, Lotta performed with local companies. Traveling cut into her rehearsal time with cast members. She practiced with them for only a few days before the performance. The actors and actresses gossiped about her, saying she was a slow study. From the beginning of her career, ever since she was a Fairy Star performing for miners, she had struggled to memorize her lines. Sometimes she forgot them on stage. When that happened, Lotta made up new ones, grabbed her banjo and sang, or laughed. She said, "Might as well when you can't cover up a thing. I like to laugh anyway." Lotta kept wondering if she would be able to play serious parts in shows. Then one day she watched a famous actress in a sad role. Lotta decided that if she ever

In the late 1860s, most train travelers slept in their seats. Some long distance trains included sleeping cars. They looked like regular passenger cars. But at night, porters lowered berths from the ceiling, unfolded the seats, and made up the beds. Curtains hanging from the ceiling provided some privacy.

Passengers brought their own food to eat on the train or ate in eating houses at water stops. The houses were located where the steam trains took on wood and water. Occasionally, robbers held up travelers in these isolated spots. Later, railroads provided dining cars on their trains so people could eat in a safe place.

had to say depressing words onstage, she would giggle.

As Lotta toured, generous fans gave her flowers, gold watches, and jewelry. Mary Ann added the valuables to Lotta's growing collection, but she only wore the jewelry onstage or for photographs. She had no time for friendships or vacations. If Lotta played in one place for a few weeks, her brothers might join her and her parents.

In a letter to an elderly San Francisco friend, Lotta wrote about theater people treating her with respect. "I'm a star!" Lotta said. "Yes, really I am!" Despite this, Lotta missed California. She pictured herself opening that summer at Maguire's Opera House and performing in Sacramento and Nevada. But this wasn't the time for Lotta to go West— New York tempted her again.

Thoughts about her failure there kept crossing Lotta's mind as she traveled from city to city. She stared out of train windows, rocking and swaying. Over wooden bridges, the trains clattered. Rivers, trees, and farms rolled by. Workers in fields waved, and the train whistles shrieked. What could she do to impress New Yorkers? They were used to the best entertainers in the world. Perhaps she needed to better showcase her talents. Lotta remembered how she had made the miners laugh and decided to try something new when she performed.

Lotta spiced her dialogue with small, funny movements. She twisted her face, smirked, shrugged, and winked. There were still no women comedians at this time, but audiences laughed during her performance. She packed the theaters, and reporters wrote glowing reviews.

Lotta and Mary Ann pondered what to do next. If only they could find a play with a funny character that danced, sang, and played the banjo. After some searching, Mary Ann found a playwright who could create one.

John Brougham was an actor who also wrote plays. For Lotta, he created *Little Nell and the Marchioness*. He based his play on the popular novel *The Olde Curiosity Shop* by Charles Dickens. Brougham's character Nell, a starving teenage servant, suffers under terrible working conditions. In contrast, the merry Marchioness, a young noblewoman, enjoys the good life. Lotta would take both roles. Mary Ann bought the play.

In Boston, Massachusetts, Lotta hired a company of local actors and actresses and tried the play out several times. After a few changes were made, Lotta declared she was ready to perform in New York. In the summer of 1867, she arrived in the city. Three years had passed since her unsuccessful debut. This time, her mama rented Wallack's, an elegant theater. Lotta hired and rehearsed with a large company of the best actors and actresses, dancers, and singers. Playbills hailed Lotta as

The best-selling English author Charles Dickens lived from 1812 to 1870. When he was twelve, his father didn't pay his debts and was sent to prison. Charles left school and worked in a factory to earn money for his family until his father returned. He had to leave school again when he was fifteen to work in an office to help his family. His experiences helped him write many stories about the poor and made the public aware of the difficult lives of orphans and working children. His characters encountered dirty cities, disease, and unemployment. In the 1860s, many Americans knew about Charles Dickens's sad novel *The Olde Curiosity Shop* about pitiful little Nell and her poor grandfather who had gambled and lost all their money.

"The California Wonder." The show would open in August.

On opening night in her hot, stuffy dressing room, twenty-year-old Lotta wore a faded, ragged cotton dress and dirty apron. She pulled on her worn leather boots with no laces and stood up. Waving her fan, she paced. She tried to push the memories from the last time she played in New York City to the back of her mind. But she worried she might fail again. Reviews would be printed in newspapers across the country. Everyone would know! Perhaps she would always be The California Favorite and nothing more. "I had no confidence in myself," Lotta later admitted.

Backstage, Mary Ann chattered while Lotta messed up her hair and smudged a piece of burned cork under her eyes. The audience buzzed as they settled themselves in the theater. Lotta opened the dressing room door and strode down the hall to the wings. Actors, actresses, and stagehands carrying props bustled by. Lotta tried to get into character. She frowned and thought, "I'm poor Little Nell, and very, very serious . . . I'm poor Little Nell . . . *poor Little Nell*." She walked across the stage and sat down at a table.

Light applause spilled over the gaslights as the curtain rose. All of Lotta's doubts disappeared. She stared at the hunk of meat that rested on the table. Later in the first act, Lotta exited the stage. She returned in a lovely, stylish dress as the Marchioness character. She chuckled, sang, strummed her banjo, and sparkled as she danced across the stage in the arms of a male actor.

When the final curtain fell, Lotta and the cast bowed as waves of applause and cheers filled the theater. The audience had experienced something new—a play with a plot, comedy, and music performed by a rising star.

LOTTA.

Houseworth's Celebrities.   12 Montgomery St., San Francisco.

Lotta, by Thomas Houseworth, 1872-1893. Here she is wearing her costume from *Little Nell and the Marchioness.* (Macauley's Theatre Collection, 1980.20.0325, Archives and Special Collections, Ekstrom Library, University of Louisville, http://digital.library.louisville.edu/cdm/ref/collection/macauley/id/331)

A theater critic said, "Lotta's face as she sits on the kitchen table, eyeing the dreadful mutton-bone, haunts me." Another said Lotta acted "sweet and tender as 'Little Nell,' saucey and tough as the 'Marchioness' . . . and she has earned her right to be considered an actress and an artist." "I was pretty proud, of course," Lotta recalled, "when I had a New York success for the first time."

The show ran for five weeks, and Lotta earned thousands of dollars. But she longed for more than one big hit. She and her parents left New York and went on tour.

Lotta added more dancing and liked to change her lines when performing in *Little Nell and the Marchioness* and other plays. She had fun breaking theater traditions and took men's roles, wore trousers, and smoked cigars.

The star created lively characters by adding funny actions to her roles. She lifted herself onto tables, swung her feet and showed her legs, kicked, skipped, and rolled off sofas. She hardly ever stood still. One actor said, "In 'Little Nell' she was serious, and played with feeling; but she was born to make us laugh, and not to weep." Sometimes Lotta spoke with an English or Irish accent, made up jokes, and poked fun at everything. Audiences crowded into theaters to see the petite performer.

Lotta now received a share of the profit from ticket sales, but theater owners always paid Mary Ann. She still controlled the family's funds. She gave Crabtree an allowance—just enough so he could dress well and not have too much left over to buy liquor. Sometimes when they visited a city, Lotta received party invitations that included her parents. She couldn't count on Crabtree to show up and never knew when he might appear drunk.

When they toured, Mary Ann put Lotta's earnings inside a strong trunk, locked it, and kept the key. She deposited

Lotta, by Gilbert & Bacon, date unknown (Macauley's Theatre Collection, 1980.20.0311, Archives and Special Collections, Ekstrom Library, University of Louisville, http://digital.library.louisville.edu/cdm/ref/collection/macauley/id/317)

the money in a New York bank at the end of the trip. But late one spring evening in St. Louis, Missouri, Crabtree pried the large case open. He stole $35,000 in cash.

That night, Crabtree slept at a hotel. The clerk noticed Lotta's father had been drinking. The next morning, Crabtree left the city by train.

Lotta felt hurt. How could her papa steal money she had earned for the family? He was not only a drunk but also a thief! And she worried about him. She wondered where he had gone and why he didn't come back.

Chapter 7

Tragedies and Triumphs

Newspapers printed the story about John Crabtree stealing his famous daughter's money and disappearing. One headline declared, "A Young Actress in Distress." The article said Lotta believed her father will "turn up all right" in time.

The evening after Crabtree stole the money, Lotta prepared at the theater for her show but hardly talked to anyone. Pulling herself together, she managed to perform as usual and delighted the audience.

Days passed, and her father did not return. Then New York City police spotted Crabtree stepping off a train. They brought him to the station house and notified Mary Ann. Mama and Lotta rushed into the courtroom as Crabtree stood before a judge.

Lotta told the judge that her papa "had not wronged her out of a penny." Police informed the judge that Crabtree had all the missing funds on him when he got off the train. Everyone looked at Lotta. She refused to accuse her father of a crime. Crabtree promised to give Lotta all of the stolen money, and the judge set him free. Lotta and her parents left the station house together.

But Crabtree didn't return the money. Mary Ann told the New York police to arrest him and put him in jail, which they did. Newspapers across the country blazed with the continuing story, and Lotta hid from the public. When Crabtree finally returned the cash, the police released him. Mary Ann paid her husband a bigger allowance and made him agree to give up all claims to their daughter's money. Crabtree continued to live with the family but didn't travel as much with Lotta and his wife.

Three months later, Lotta received another shock. While she was performing in Philadelphia, Pennsylvania, her mother received a message sent by telegraph. Lotta's youngest brother, George, age thirteen, was in a hospital in Buffalo, New York. He had run away from boarding school and tried to hop onto a passing freight car. He reached out, fell, and the wheels ran over his leg. Lotta cancelled her performance, and she and Mary Ann rushed to George's bedside.

George's leg was removed below the knee to save his life. While he recovered, the family planned a trip to California. Four years had passed since they left San Francisco. Touring and the long, difficult journey by way of Panama had kept Lotta away. Now she wanted to see the West on the new Transcontinental Railroad. Her mother made arrangements for appearances in Salt Lake City, which was in Utah Territory, and in San Francisco.

In the early summer of 1869, the Crabtree family left New York. Mary Ann had bought first-class train tickets, and they rode in a comfortable sleeper car and ate in a dining car. Lotta enjoyed being with her papa and her brothers. She watched the landscape change from big, crowded Eastern cities to scattered Midwestern farms. The train rolled across the flat, grassy plains and into the rugged Rocky Mountains, climbing and twisting through canyons and steaming by tumbling streams.

In Salt Lake City, Utah, Lotta and her mother got off the train. They would join Crabtree and her brothers later in San Francisco. Lotta and a local cast rehearsed in the large, luxurious Salt Lake Theatre. Brigham Young, the leader of the Mormon Church, was a patron. He wanted the public to enjoy good entertainment and music—but he didn't like tragic plays.

Lotta worried before the play opened. If Brigham Young didn't approve of the show, people would not come to her other performances. But her humor and funny movements made him and the audience laugh. Over the next few days, many tickets were sold. Mary Ann was pleased when she collected Lotta's earnings before they boarded a train for California.

The Transcontinental Railroad line ended in Sacramento. Lotta and her mother transferred to a steamboat and sailed down the sunny Sacramento River. Lotta remembered when she was six and steamed up that river on a similar boat to meet her papa. Now she was returning to San Francisco as a star, and she thought about the plays she would appear in. Leading actors and actresses she had worked with as a teenager would have supporting roles. She wondered how they would treat her, and she hoped that San Franciscan audiences would enjoy her comedy like they had in the past.

Lotta opened *Little Nell and the Marchioness* in San Francisco on August 1, 1869. The experienced cast performed well, and Lotta commanded every scene. All eyes were on her as soon as she stepped onstage. A theatre critic wrote, Lotta "is a curious little witch . . . brim full of all kinds of antics. The welcome she received was a hearty one, of which she seemed delighted."

For six weeks, the twenty-two-year-old star acted in different plays. She also sang, danced, played her banjo, and even rode a horse in one role. Bearded miners in leather boots who remembered her as a Fairy Star traveled from Gold Country to see her perform. The days when they bet their gold in card games in the city's saloons were over. Now people gambled in stocks. Businesses had grown, and

> In 1856, a telegraph company worked on developing a new way to deliver messages. An operator used a telegraph key that started and stopped the flow of electricity. He tapped a round, flat knob to make short and long signals that stood for letters and numbers. Each letter and number was represented by a different combination of these signals. A wire carried the signals to another operator, who listened to the clicks and converted them into words, which they wrote on paper.
>
> By 1861, the company had joined other telegraph businesses and had taken the name Western Union. That year, the new corporation finished stringing wires from poles across the country. Communications could now be sent from coast to coast in a day! At Western Union offices, operators gave the brief paper messages to errand boys to deliver to companies and homes.

In May 1869 at Promontory Summit in Utah Territory, a worker pounded the final spike into railroad tracks joining two lines. The Central Pacific Railroad had begun in Sacramento, California, and the Union Pacific Railroad had started in Council Bluffs, Iowa. As officials and workers cheered, a telegraph operator tapped the news in a message for Pres. Ulysses S. Grant in Washington, DC. Americans celebrated! The days of paying over $1,500 for an uncomfortable weeks-long ride in many stagecoaches were over. Instead, a train ticket for travel from New York to California cost $150—a tenth of the price—and the trip lasted just ten days. The Transcontinental Railroad carried both people and goods. It united the East and West Coasts, expanded the economy, and spurred development of the West.

mansions ringed the top of Nob Hill. In the new, luxurious California Theater, the pioneers joined jeweled ladies, firemen, policemen, and city and business leaders. One night when Lotta gave a benefit, the audience rewarded her with a gold and diamond wreath for her hair and a package filled with gold coins.

At one of Lotta's last performances on that trip, she received many curtain calls. Numerous bouquets were tossed on the stage. She thanked her fans for the flowers and praised the cast and the theater. She promised to return the next year, saying she would be "improved and more deserving the applause of her friends."

For Lotta, San Francisco was home. It was where she had lived the longest, polished her skills, and received opportunities for success. Her aunt and cousins lived there, too, and she enjoyed being with them again. But by the

Lotta, circa 1879 (Macauley's Theatre Collection, 1980.20.0486, Archives and Special Collections, Ekstrom Library, University of Louisville, http://digital.library.louisville.edu/cdm/ref/collection/macauley/id/491)

middle of September, she left the city with her parents and brothers and once again crossed America on the Transcontinental Railroad. She had engagements for the upcoming season.

During the winter and spring, as Lotta toured, the Crabtrees planned a trip to England. She wished she could go right then and there! At last, in June 1870, the family left New York on an ocean liner; they arrived in England seven days later. Lotta's parents were born there, and she enjoyed meeting their old friends and relatives. She was now twenty-three years old, and this was her first vacation from working since she was eight. At summer's end, the Crabtrees returned to America, and Lotta resumed touring.

Lotta often played clever kid characters who survived by their wits. Working children adored her. She gave them Christmas presents and free tickets to her shows. She also helped raise money for a shelter for orphans of sailors and gave benefits to support housing for homeless children.

During the first of many annual trips to New Orleans,

In those days, poor children only attended school for a few years. Parents expected them to help by working on farms, in businesses, or for wealthy families. Abandoned and orphaned children with no friends or families to care for them lived on the streets. Mostly boys, they found jobs shining shoes, running errands, or selling newspapers for a penny or two of profit. In several cities, private institutions provided them with a safe place to sleep, as well as some food, clothing, shoes, and education. In 1866, the Children's Aid Society in New York took care of 12,500 homeless children in different lodging houses.

Newsgirl & Boy Selling around Saloon Entrances, Bowery, Location: New York, New York, by Lewis Wickes Hine, 1910. Lotta encountered many working children such as these. (Library of Congress)

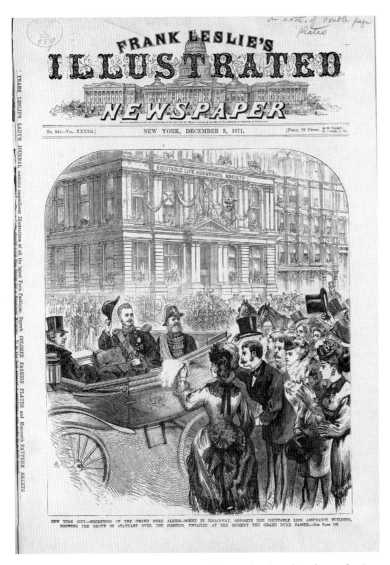

FRANK LESLIE'S
ILLUSTRATED
NEWSPAPER

No. 845—Vol. XXXIII] NEW YORK, DECEMBER 9, 1871. [Price, 10 Cents.

NEW YORK CITY—RECEPTION OF THE GRAND DUKE ALEXIS—SCENE IN BROADWAY, OPPOSITE THE EQUITABLE LIFE ASSURANCE BUILDING,
SHOWING THE GROUP OF STATUARY OVER THE PORTICO, UNVAILED AT THE MOMENT THE GRAND DUKE PASSED.—See Page 198.

The Grand Duke Alexis in a carriage, tipping his hat, during a reception in New York City, from *Frank Leslie's Illustrated Newspaper*, December 9, 1871 (Library of Congress)

Louisiana, Lotta handed out clothes to newsboys. Soon they ran after her carriage shouting her name whenever they saw her and crowded around the stage doors of theaters to thank her. She also provided baseball uniforms and equipment so the newsboys could have a team. They called it "Lotta's Baseball Club" and made her an honorary member. At a benefit she gave to raise money for the Newsboys Home, the boys presented her with a bouquet of flowers and a gold medal. When one of the boys handed them to her, Lotta kissed him on the cheek—embarrassing him and delighting the audience. With tears in her eyes, she clutched the medal and told the crowd she couldn't find words to express her feelings.

In the spring of 1872, the young, tall, and handsome Grand Duke Alexis of Russia arrived in New Orleans as part of his visit to America. New York City had given him a grand parade and reception. In Washington, DC, he had received a welcome at the White House.

In New Orleans, the Grand Duke enjoyed Mardi Gras. During the carnival celebrations, he saw Lotta perform. He could not understand English, but she enchanted him nonetheless. After they were introduced, he invited her to a banquet on his ship, and Lotta accepted. During the meal, the Grand Duke allowed each of the ship's officers to take turns sitting by her side. Petite Lotta charmed them all. Back in her hotel, Lotta told her mama about the marvelous time she had. She kept thinking about the Grand Duke and hoped she would see him again.

Chapter 8

On the Road Again

Grand Duke Alexis sailed away without contacting Lotta, and she eventually learned that the yacht she had been on didn't even belong to him. The US government had loaned the vessel to the Grand Duke for his visit to America. Lotta and Mary Ann left New Orleans for the next stop on their tour of the South. Days later, Lotta received a telegram from the Grand Duke saying he had ordered a present to be sent to her. When it arrived, she admired the lovely diamond, opal, and pearl bracelet. Her mama put it in the large leather satchel she carried when traveling. It held the gifts of jewelry Lotta had received, which she still only wore on the stage. Lotta did not see the Grand Duke again.

In the fall of 1872, the Crabtrees traveled to England, as Lotta's father had decided to retire there on her mother's allowance. George, age sixteen, and Jack, eighteen, settled into English boarding schools. Then Lotta and Mary Ann crossed the English Channel to France. In Paris, Mary Ann rented an apartment, and Lotta studied French and the piano.

"When we go abroad," Lotta said later, "I never go sightseeing; when we reach our destination I am entertained by everything and everybody about me. I do go to the art galleries, but that's all."

Along the streets of Paris, Lotta found galleries exhibiting colorful art by painters who were called Impressionists. She signed up for art lessons and discovered that she liked painting "as well as acting."

In the spring, Lotta and her mother returned to England and rented a house. George and Jack joined them during school vacations. Neighbors sometimes spotted the pretty twenty-seven-year-old star driving a pony cart. They said she looked like she was seventeen.

Lotta did not perform while she was in England. She took the longest break from entertaining of her career—almost a year. The public noticed her absence, and during the summer Lotta read reports in the newspapers that she was dead or dying! She decided it was time to return to work. She said goodbye to her papa, and she, her mama, and her brothers traveled by steamship back to America.

Mary Ann set up the new season as Lotta read scripts from playwrights who had created characters to fit her personality. In those days, actors had to be flexible and perform in many roles. Lotta appeared in at least twelve plays a year, often taking two parts in each. Soon she was once again touring, performing to sold-out houses. Sometimes at the end of an act, the spectators kept applauding after she had left the stage and the curtain had dropped. They hoped she would return. Instead, she pushed her tiny ankle out from behind the cloth and tapped her toe. Seeing a woman's ankle in those days was rare. Audiences went wild and could hardly wait for the next act to begin.

In 1875, Lotta thanked San Franciscans for helping make her a success by sending them a $10,000, fancy, bronzed, cast-iron drinking fountain. The bronze surface glowed like a new copper penny. The twenty-one-foot structure held four basins on the side. Black tin cups hung nearby on a chain. Below them, two smaller containers provided water for thirsty dogs and horses. City leaders placed Lotta's Fountain on busy Market Street.

Two years later, Lotta stopped at the fountain while she was on a Western tour. She sipped a drink of water, smiled, and waved to onlookers before stepping into her carriage

The Lotta Fountain, San Francisco, California, 1880, photograph by T. E. Hecht (San Francisco History Center, San Francisco Public Library)

and traveling into the Sierra Nevada Mountains. Mary Ann bought a gold mine, and she and Lotta visited Rabbit Creek. Lotta fondly remembered living there when she was eight. She thought back on her dancing lessons with Mart Taylor and her debut before the miners in the small log cabin theater. Now she entertained in magnificent theaters for thousands of people at a time.

Across the country, people danced the Lotta Galop and the Lotta Polka. Throughout her thirties, Lotta continued to ride a wave of popularity. After seeing her perform, the famous actress Helena Modjeska said, "She infused life into the part and her realism was simply wonderful."

Everyone who worked with Lotta respected her. W. H. Crane, who played opposite her in *Little Nell and the Marchioness*, said that if the audience didn't react, "she never thought that it could be anyone's fault but her own." But if after a few performances the audience responded well, she would smile and thank the cast for putting energy into the show.

Lotta toured most of the year, but for several summers she and her family vacationed in Newport, Rhode Island. In the popular vacation spot, millionaires had built mansions overlooking the ocean. Mary Ann rented a spacious cottage, and the family enjoyed rowing, sailing, and bathing along the town's sandy shores.

Twenty miles away, Lotta's brothers worked at a company that traded stocks. Her mother owned a percentage of the business. Young, carefree, and careless, George and Jack dressed well and told amusing stories. One day, Jack decided to seek his fortune in Arizona. His mother gave him a tent and camping equipment and bought part of a livery stable in Tombstone for him to run. But Jack argued with his business partner and returned a year later.

Lotta Crabtree, 1876 (San Francisco History Center, San Francisco Public Library)

Jack, Mary Ann, and Lotta Crabtree in San Francisco, circa 1879 (Courtesy Lake Hopatcong Historical Museum, Landing, New Jersey)

Hundreds of young men wished they could get to know Lotta. Fans gathered at the doors of hotels and theaters hoping to catch a glimpse of her as she dashed from place to place. Reports circulated about the star's romances with several possible suitors, her engagement, and her marriage. But the rumors fizzled. The press called her "The Unapproachable." Reporters begged for interviews, but Mary Ann kept them away.

Before every performance, Lotta napped in her hotel room. Outside the door, her mama sat in a chair. "Shh!" she hissed when noisy guests passed by.

In 1883, Lotta arrived in London, England, for her first European appearance and received a surprise. Minnie Palmer, an American entertainer in her twenties, had been performing in London. She was a hit performing Lotta's favorite parts and imitating the star's actions and styles. Since Londoners didn't know this, they would think that Lotta, now age thirty-six, was copying Minnie.

For her first show, Lotta chose a play set in England and took the role of the fourteen-year-old gypsy, Little Bright Eyes. She had performed this part successfully for five years in America. A few days before Christmas, *Musette* opened. From the beginning, every actor was booed, their words interrupted. In one scene, an evil nobleman chased sweet Little Bright Eyes through the countryside. Then the audience's ridicule increased into a "hurricane of catcalls, of loud guffaws, of insulting sneers." But Lotta persisted and finished the act.

The crowd shouted, and the curtain dropped, ending the play early. Lotta rushed to her dressing room past her mama, stagehands, and performers. Streaks of black mascara stained her rosy cheeks. Not since her New York debut at age sixteen had she suffered such humiliation.

What had she done wrong? Why didn't they laugh? What could she do to change things by the next performance tomorrow night?

In her dressing room, Lotta sobbed. She thought her career was over and no one would ever come to see her perform again! Backstage, the cast members waited and whispered. The stage manager called off the party planned for after the play. Lotta and Mary Ann fled to their hotel in a carriage through the dark streets. The horse's hooves clattered over the cobblestones as the star brooded.

The following day, Lotta read the unfavorable reviews in the London newspapers. She cancelled *Musette*. She also had an idea.

Lotta and the cast plunged into rehearsals for *Little Nell and the Marchioness*. Sixteen years before in New York, the play had catapulted her to stardom; perhaps it would do the same for her in England. As Lotta prepared for opening night, she tinkered with her two roles and worried. Would the English like it? If they didn't, what would happen to her career? American newspapers had carried the news of her failed London debut. She must do well this time.

In her dressing room on a cold evening in January 1884, Lotta slipped on her costume. As the curtain rose, light applause greeted her. Lotta fell into the familiar role of the dirty, hungry servant that she had played so many times before. Later in the act, when she emerged as the lovely Marchioness in a fancy dress, she danced back and forth with short, rapid movements while laughter filled the theater. A critic said it was "the funniest thing ever done in comic dancing."

Lotta moved close to the footlights and sat down in a chair, revealing her pink petticoats, silk stockings, and high-heeled shoes. She looked over the lights at the audience and

In the 1880s, Italian immigrant musicians brought the mandolin to America. Some formed musical groups and played their small, stringed instruments to enthusiastic crowds. People found the inexpensive instrument easy to learn, and it became wildly popular.

smiled. Usually at this point of the performance, she would play the banjo, but she decided to do something different.

Instead of a banjo, she grabbed a mandolin. Lotta's small fingers strummed its strings, and her warm voice filled the large theater with song. When she finished, people rose to their feet, shouting approval and applauding.

Smiling and bowing, a relieved Lotta stood before the cheering crowd. Afterwards, she and the cast celebrated at a reception backstage. Across town, Minnie Palmer learned of Lotta's success and planned what she would do next.

Chapter 9

Ups and Downs

Minnie Palmer continued performing the roles that made Lotta famous. The young actress kicked higher and raised her skirts. The two rivals packed theaters for months, and both English and American newspapers carried details of the battle. Because Minnie had appeared in England first, Londoners considered her performances as original and Lotta's as imitations.

Thirty years later, the actress Helena Modjeska wrote about the incident in her memoir and said, "Such proceedings as stealing somebody's artistic creation are unpardonable, yet they happen often . . . happily there are many recording angels among the audience and in the press. The shallow imitators usually disappear from the surface, as it happened in this case." By 1910, the public had forgotten Minnie Palmer's name. Helena Modjeska went on to say that Lotta's name, on the other hand, "will never be forgotten by any one [*sic*] who saw her on the stage."

Lotta and Mary Ann returned to New York for the new season. At thirty-six, the star worried that critics and fans would think she was getting too old to perform. So she danced with more enthusiasm and created new bits of action and comedy.

In *Ma'amzelle Nitouche*, she played a Japanese opera singer and wore a silk kimono. In one scene, she fluttered her fan and darted around the stage with a pink lampshade on her head, delighting the audience. One critic said, "She is original. No one resembles her except her imitators."

Edward Sothern, one of the best comic actors of the day, saw Lotta perform and sent her a note. He wrote that when she came onstage, the lights were brilliant. When she went off, "it seemed as if the gas were turned down." He praised her natural acting, saying it made the rest of the cast "seem like mere actors."

Lotta now toured with her own company. The entertainers traveled in a separate railroad car away from other passengers. One of the actresses said, "Lotta is a dear little soul. I can get on with her admirably. But the mamma! Oh, dear me, I cannot endure her!" Theater managers called Mary Ann a terror, but she continued as Lotta's business manager. Lotta hired the actors and actresses and produced her plays. At the time, men performed this job.

Before Lotta's performances, she preferred not to rehearse with the cast. The actress didn't think she was superior to them, but she said sometimes she got an idea onstage and wanted to act spontaneously. It was hard on

Lotta, by Napoleon Sarony, 1871-1896 (Macauley's Theatre Collection, 1980.20.0303, Archives and Special Collections, Ekstrom Library, University of Louisville, http://digital.library.louisville.edu/cdm/ref/collection/macauley/id/310)

the other actors and actresses when Lotta departed from the script, but they didn't complain. She treated them well and always paid them. An elderly stagehand who knew Lotta for a long time said, "Other actresses came from the stage tired and disgusted with their work, but with Lotta, it all seemed play and therefore pleased her."

Away from the theater, Lotta used stage makeup. Most actresses did not. Women gossiped that Lotta sprinkled cayenne pepper in her hair to make it gleam in the footlights. Offstage, the aging star often wore a girlish, plain cotton dress with a wide sash tied in a big bow in the back. Petite Mary Ann appeared in fashionable satin dresses and wraps decorated with black lace and beadwork. A black lace bonnet and soft, black leather gloves completed her outfit.

In 1885, Lotta's mother ordered the construction of a house at Lake Hopatcong in northwest New Jersey. Easterners escaped hot cities in the summer and sought refuge and recreation on New Jersey's largest lake. Real estate agents boasted that the temperature was ten degrees cooler than back in the city—and there were few mosquitoes. Located forty-five miles from New York City, Lake Hopatcong was less than two hours away by train. Fares cost $1.30 for one-way rides and $2.05 round trip.

Lotta's mother furnished the house's eighteen rooms and hired a butler and a maid. She named the three-story house Attol Tryst. ("Attol" is Lotta spelled backwards.) Mary Ann paid for the house with Lotta's money and gave it to her daughter. The actress was almost forty, and Attol Tryst was her first permanent home since she left San Francisco as a teenager.

Vines climbed the building's walls, and a verandah looked upon a sloping green lawn and a boathouse. At a dock, a steamboat waited. Mary Ann named the vessel

Lotta. During the summertime, Lotta and her brothers rode bicycles or horses, played billiards, and drove their mama in a carriage to neighbors' parties. But the roads were few, and they usually traveled around the lake by boat. In the *Lotta* or a rowboat, they passed cabins, hotels, lodges, and mansions on their way to small islands for picnics.

Around Lotta's cottage, she spotted quail dashing from bush to bush, rabbits, raccoons, and squirrels. Eagles surveyed it all from the treetops. And on hot summer days, she and her guests enjoyed bathing in the lake's crystal waters. Lotta entertained old theater friends and gave masquerade balls. But often she slipped away from the visitors and found a quiet place to paint, her new hobby.

In the fall, Lotta and her mother left on another tour. Pres. Benjamin Harrison attended two of her plays that season. After leaving Washington, DC, the Crabtree women toured the West.

Cottage of Miss Lotta, Lake Hopatcong, New Jersey, date unknown (Courtesy Lake Hopatcong Historical Museum, Landing, New Jersey)

In the 1890s, people used the word "bathing" to describe swimming. Before taking a dip in lakes or the ocean, they followed common practices. They used bathing houses to change from their street clothes into bathing suits. Ladies wore bathing slippers to protect their feet from glass, oyster shells, and rocks. As many women as men went into the water. A good time to bathe was 11 a.m., but even better was 4 to 5 p.m. Doctors recommended waiting at least three hours after eating so the meal could be digested.

Around Virginia City, Nevada, prospectors with white beards remembered their Fairy Star. They poured out of the foothills and packed the theater. Lotta sang the old songs, played her banjo, danced jigs and reels, joked, and slid on her tummy across the stage. At the end of the show, the men stomped their leather boots, hollered, and whooped like they did when she was a girl.

When the performance was over, the miners gathered around the stage door waiting for Lotta. She emerged, waved, and stepped into her carriage. The men unhooked the horses and pulled it and the smiling star to her hotel while singing, "Lotta! Lotta! Like no other!"

In the spring of 1891, Lotta fell onstage during a show. In great pain, she limped off. She had broken several bones in her back. Her mother cancelled the rest of the season and took Lotta to Attol Tryst. Usually active, Lotta didn't like lying on her back and resting. She stared out the window as birds sang in the budding trees. Would she ever perform again? Were other actresses taking her place? Was her career over?

Summer passed, and as the green leaves turned to copper,

orange, and red, Lotta received tragic news. George, age thirty-five, had died suddenly on an ocean liner crossing the Atlantic. Lotta was stunned. She was fond of her youngest brother and remembered their happy times together. The incident also made her think about her own life and how many years she had left to do what she truly longed to do.

While Lotta healed, the postman delivered sacks of fan letters wishing her a speedy recovery. One note came from a former New Orleans newsboy who had now grown up. Lotta didn't have a secretary and answered her mail herself. She wrote to him, "It will be months before I play again. If it did not give me pleasure I would not go on again."

Winter crawled by, and Lotta's back pain lessened. She couldn't wait any longer to perform! Early in 1892, she resumed touring. She longed to bounce around the stage like before her fall, but her back ached. Was it time to stop entertaining? She had performed since she was eight, and it was hard to let go—she loved her fans. Lotta wished her back would feel better soon. However, with every passing day, the pain increased. It *was* time.

Lotta Crabtree announced she was retiring from the stage. At age forty-four, she topped the list of the richest American actresses. Her mother had purchased dozens of plots of land in different cities in addition to a horse stable, theater, and a gold mine—all in her daughter's name. Yet Lotta didn't care about money. Other things were more important to her.

Now that Lotta had retired, rumors spread that she was to marry, and a fan wrote her asking if it were true. She answered, "My little mother is my delightful companion. It is late in the day for me to think of marriage. I am the very happiest little old maid you can find."

The next year, Crabtree visited Attol Tryst. When he arrived,

Lotta, photograph by Gilbert & Bacon, 1880s or 1890s (Macauley's Theatre Collection, 1980.20.0324, Archives and Special Collections, Ekstrom Library, University of Louisville, http://digital.library. louisville.edu/cdm/ref/collection/macauley/id/330)

Lotta noticed that her seventy-five-year-old father looked unwell. The family enjoyed being together again, and her parents acted like friends and didn't argue. On a cold December day, Lotta kissed her papa goodbye, and he sailed back to England.

The actress celebrated New Year's Eve and hoped 1894 would be a good year. During the first week of January, she received a telegram. Soon after arriving home, Crabtree had died. The news shocked Lotta. He had been with her only a short time before. Tears filled her eyes. First George, now her papa. And her father had died alone, so far from the family.

Eventually, Lotta's back healed. Now that she wasn't performing, she discovered a new experience. For the first time in her life, she had time for herself. She and her mama lived at either Attol Tryst or a New York hotel. Later on, her brother Jack joined them on a trip to Europe and Africa.

Once in a while, Lotta granted an interview. When a reporter asked Lotta about her early touring days in California, she described them as an "adventure." Another time, someone questioned her about how she spent her days in retirement. Lotta answered, "I paint. That keeps me perfectly happy . . . I wish I were a landscape painter when I look out of that window, but no—portraits." The journalist asked if she ever thought about returning to the stage. Lotta admitted, "Sometimes. When it does I go to the theater and have the pleasure of seeing others act."

Now in her fifties, Lotta looked like a thirty-year-old. But her mother, with her silver curls, aged rapidly. Guests to their New York hotel suite often noticed Mary Ann sitting and jingling a pile of coins in her lap. She also liked to tell stories about their touring days and exaggerated the details.

After her mama died in 1905 at the age of eighty-five, Lotta declared, "What I am, what I have been, I owe entirely to my mother. My mother was the most wonderful woman that ever lived and I want the world to know it!"

Lotta felt uneasy as she faced life without her mother. What would she do now?

Chapter 10

The Golden Years

Months after her mother's death, Lotta decided to try the horse racing business. She gave her brother Jack an allowance and made him manager of her stable. Soon she owned about twenty racehorses. When asked what she liked about horses, Lotta said, "I love to see the beautiful things flash by so swiftly mile after mile and all without apparent effort."

Almost sixty years old, the actress drove herself to racetracks in her large, red automobile with the canvas top folded down. She named the car the Red Rose. At the time, proper ladies did not drive cars powered by gasoline.

With a new, short haircut and wearing stylish, shorter skirts, Lotta stood beside her horses before they raced. She stroked their necks and spoke softly to them. Many were winners and appeared at events from New England to the South.

Once after spraining her ankle, Lotta sat in her car at a Lexington, Kentucky, racetrack and watched her horse win. She couldn't walk, so while six thousand people cheered, her companions carried her to the grandstand. They placed her among the roses of a large floral horseshoe, and she listened to a singer who was performing. Lotta presented the flowers to the young performer with a note: "From one artiste to another with the love of Lotta."

Lotta now lived in Massachusetts to be near her racehorses. On April 18, 1906, newsboys around the country waved their papers and cried, "Earthquake rocks San Francisco!" Lotta searched her own paper. She read

Lotta's Fountain at the intersection of Geary, Kearny, and Market Streets, 1906 (San Francisco History Center, San Francisco Public Library)

about buildings tumbling, walls cracking, streets sinking, and fires raging in the city and surrounding area. She knew those places! She learned that many animals and people had died or were injured, and she wondered about the people she knew. Were they alive or hurt? Were the theaters destroyed? And what happened to her fountain?

Later, Lotta learned her bronzed fountain had survived and stood surrounded by ruins on Market Street. She smiled when she found out it now performed a new function; people left messages at Lotta's Fountain for missing family members and friends and many times met one another there.

By now, Lotta's horse-racing business was losing money, and she didn't like the way Jack ran the stable. He wasted money, hired assistants, and took too many vacations with his wife. Lotta thought about selling the stable, but she loved horses and being around them. Then several of her favorites injured themselves and could no longer race. She missed cheering them on and the excitement at the races, so she sold the stables.

Lotta also sold Attol Tryst. She found it difficult to vacation there as she kept remembering her happy summers with George and her parents. But now they were gone.

In 1909, Lotta bought the Brewster Hotel in Boston, Massachusetts, and moved into a suite. At the end of the hall, a room held her trunks of costumes, shelves with hatboxes, old shoes, boxes of play scripts, scrapbooks filled with newspaper clippings, photos, and programs. Jack worked as hotel manager for a while until his bad business decisions once again cost her money. They quarreled, and he and his wife moved to North Carolina. Lotta hired a new manager, and soon many entertainers said Lotta's hotel was their favorite place to stay when they visited the city.

With good people running her hotel, Lotta left for a vacation in 1912. On a dock in Boston Harbor, a reporter spotted the small sixty-five-year-old entertainer. He described her for his readers as "girlish" with a "well rounded figure, a pretty, beautiful expressive face, a rose and cream complexion and brownish golden hair." He asked Lotta why she was successful.

Lotta replied, "My secret, I think, to all success is naturalness and sincerity. If a girl is going to truly succeed in the world she must be her own self." And with a smile, the star boarded an ocean liner and sailed to Europe.

In Paris, France, Lotta ate in cafés, wandered the crooked and narrow streets, dropped into art galleries, visited art museums, enjoyed the view from the Eiffel Tower, and studied art. Her school was located in the lively Latin Quarter, a neighborhood of artists, musicians, poets, students, and writers. She fit right in and stayed for the summer.

Panorama of the Seven Bridges, Paris, France, circa 1890-1900 (Library of Congress)

Two years after Lotta returned to Boston, she received a surprising invitation from the planners of the Panama-Pacific International Exposition in San Francisco. The city wanted to show the world it had recovered from the destruction caused by the earthquake and fire. The Exposition was essentially a fair, and it would celebrate the completion of the Panama Canal linking the Atlantic and Pacific Oceans. It also would honor the Spanish explorer Vasco Núñez de Balboa's crossing of the Isthmus of Panama and reaching the Pacific Ocean four hundred years before. The planning committee wanted Lotta to give a talk on November 6, 1915—which would be Lotta Crabtree Day.

Of course, Lotta agreed! In late October, she and several friends boarded a train in New York. Traveling across the country, she wrote and memorized her speech. Along the way, she passed many places where she had entertained, and she smiled recalling those exciting times. What an adventure she had! She didn't regret one moment.

Tower of Jewels, 1915. Nighttime at the Panama Pacific International Exhibition. (Courtesy California History Room, California State Library, Sacramento, California)

The Panama-Pacific International Exposition opened on February 6, 1915, and covered 635 acres in San Francisco. For months, millions of tourists enjoyed the entertainment and attractions.

Famous people like Helen Keller, the comic movie star Charlie Chaplin, and inventor Thomas Edison attended. Laura Ingalls Wilder, who later wrote the *Little House* children's book series, described the fair grounds. "The coloring is so soft and wonderful. Blue and reds and greens and yellows and browns and grays are all blended into one without a jar anywhere. It is fairyland."

Fairgoers listened to music played on a forty-ton, 7,000 pipe organ and looked at the Liberty Bell, on loan from the City of Philadelphia. They smelled peanuts roasting, popcorn popping, and jelly scones baking. In the Joy Zone, children watched wild animals and rode a miniature train and a rollercoaster. At night, people around the hilly city came out of their houses to gaze at searchlights in rainbow colors and a dazzling fireworks show that lit up the sky over the grounds.

The fair organizers set aside certain days for specific themes, such as countries, regions, and people. Some examples were Japan Day, New England Day, Pioneer and Old Settler's Day, and Lotta Crabtree Day. The Panama-Pacific International Exposition closed on December 4, 1915.

In San Francisco on November 6, 1915, her special day, Lotta strolled the fairgrounds. During a ceremony, officials presented her with a medal and a gold nugget. At 7 p.m., she arrived at Lotta's Fountain. A band played "Home Sweet Home," and thousands of people waited for her to speak. Streetcars stopped. Lotta, dressed in yellow, matched the color of the thousand chrysanthemums decorating the grandstand. She climbed the steps to the platform, waved, and blew kisses. The crowd roared.

"My dear friends," she began—but she could not continue. Tears slipped down her wrinkled cheeks. During her long career, Lotta had never failed to perform.

"Lotta! Lotta! Lotta!" cheered the crowd, who wept with her.

After Lotta returned to Massachusetts, war broke out among European nations. Americans were divided about whether or not their country should help their allies in the battle. The actress wrote letters to newspapers pointing out that men would die, leaving widows and orphans. The United States entered the First World War in the spring of 1917, and, like most Americans, Lotta supported the war effort.

As Lotta aged, she painted pictures of herself in her performance costumes and exhibited her work at an art gallery. In the summertime, she painted by the shores of the Atlantic Ocean as seagulls soared in the salty air. At her seaside hotel, she dressed in old-fashioned clothes and dined alone. She ended the day rocking silently in a porch chair.

Lotta's brother Jack met with her at the Brewster in Boston in 1918. He returned to North Carolina and died two years later. From then on, Lotta rarely left the hotel. Friends visited, and sometimes one would take her for a drive.

Lotta Crabtree, photo taken at the Panama Pacific International Exhibition, from *Album of San Francisco* by Henry Hamilton Dobbin, circa 1920 (Courtesy California History Room, California State Library, Sacramento, California)

Lotta died on September 25, 1924, in the Brewster Hotel at the age of seventy-six. She was buried next to her mother in New York City.

Lotta never married and had no heirs. She left a $4,000,000 estate to charity (over $76,000,000 in today's dollars). In her will, she set aside $2,000,000 for disabled, sick, and wounded veterans of World War I and their dependents. Lotta said they were "the noblest and most deserving" to receive her money.

The star also provided funds for animals, the education of young women in the theater, needy actors and actresses, agricultural and music students, hospitals, and former convicts. Her gifts continue to help animals and people today.

"Charity," said Lotta, "is what is needed in this world."

Growing up in Gold Country, Lotta developed a pioneer spirit. For her whole career, she battled stage fright every time she performed. She broke theater traditions and inspired young girls and women to play the banjo. When only men were comics, she dared to perform comedy and stood as a model for future female entertainers. She was America's first comedienne.

Lotta's acting, banjo playing, dancing, humor, and singing brightened stages like glittering gold dust. With a twinkle in her eye, Fairy Star Lotta created fun and invited everyone to the good time, saying, "It is delightful to make people laugh!"

Timeline

1832	New England unions condemn child labor.
1847	Lotta Crabtree is born on November 7 in New York City.
1848	Gold is discovered in California.
1850	California becomes a state.
1853	Lotta leaves New York and arrives in San Francisco, California.
1855	Lotta joins a troupe and tours Gold Country as a Fairy Star.
1857	California Gold Rush ends as Lotta performs in San Francisco, California.
1861	The Civil War starts.
1864	Lotta leaves San Francisco and flops in her New York debut.
1864	Lotta performs in the Midwest.
1865	The Civil War ends.
1865-1867	Lotta tours the South and Northeast.
1867	Lotta dazzles New York City in *Little Nell and the Marchioness*.
1867-1891	Lotta entertains across America and in London, England.
1891	Lotta injures her back, and her brother George dies at sea.
1892	After a brief comeback, Lotta retires from the stage.
1894	Lotta's father, John Crabtree, dies in England.
1903	Striking mill children march from Philadelphia to New York to protest long hours and night work.
1906	San Francisco is shaken on April 18 by an earthquake.
1914	World War I begins.
1915	Lotta appears at the Panama-Pacific International Exposition in San Francisco on November 6, Lotta Crabtree Day.
1918	World War I ends.
1924	Lotta dies on September 25.
1938	Pres. Franklin D. Roosevelt signs the Fair Labor Standards Act, forbidding children under fourteen from performing certain jobs after school and for those under sixteen from working during school hours.

Source Notes by Chapter

Chapter 1: Ho! To California

"Crabtree must leave New York . . . ," Constance Rourke, *Troupers of the Gold Coast or the Rise of Lotta Crabtree,* Harcourt, Brace, NY, 1928, 10; "Blow, ye breezes, blow . . . ," Rodman W. Paul, *Mining Frontiers of the Far West, 1848-1880,* Holt, Rinehart, and Winston, NY, 1963, 14-15.

Chapter 2: Dancing and Singing Lessons

"I saw mining life . . . ," Jarah Comstogk, "A Personal Interview with Lotta," *San Francisco Call,* vol. 87, no. 156, May 5, 1901; "had eleven kinds of air castles . . . ," Comstogk; "We were very poor," Nan Mullenneaux, "Our Genius, Goodness, and Gumption: Child Actresses and National Identity in Mid-Nineteenth-Century America," Johns Hopkins University Press, *The Journal of the History of Childhood and Youth,* vol. 5, no. 2, Baltimore, Spring 2012, 293.

Chapter 3: A Fairy Star

"When I was through . . . ," John E. Baur, *Growing Up with California: A History of California's Children,* Kramer, Los Angeles, 1978, 280; "We used to put up in little camps . . . ," Comstogk; "I can play the banjo . . . ," Lawrence Estavan, ed., "Monographs: Lotta Crabtree, John McCullough," vol. 6, abstract from Theatre Research WPA Project 8386, San Francisco, 1938, 33; "I've a howl in my heart . . . ," Rourke, 97; "each time filling her slipper with money . . . ," Oral Coad and Edwin Mims, Jr., *The American Stage,* Yale University Press, New Haven, 1929, 183.

Chapter 4: The Early Years

"Miss Lotta, the San Francisco favorite," Linda Martin and Kerry Segrave, *Women in Comedy,* Citadel, Secaucus, NJ, 1986, 39; "the prettiest rose in the neighborhood . . . ," George R. MacMinn, *The Theater of the Golden Era in California,* Caxton, Caldwell, ID, 1941, 454; "Always I managed to pass them . . . ," MacMinn, 454; "Stay with 'em Jake . . . ," David Dempsey and Raymond Baldwin, *The Triumphs and Trials of Lotta Crabtree,* William Morrow, NY, 1968, 136; "The Battle Cry of Freedom," George F. Root, Root & Cady, Chicago, 1862; "The Bonnie Blue Flag," Harry Macarthy, A. E. Blackmar & Bro., New Orleans, 1861; "would give it [even] if they hanged her . . . ," Estavan, 40; "She faced a cold and relentless audience . . . ," Estavan, 40; "but she had sand and ginger . . . ," Baur, 282.

Chapter 5: Miss Lotty

"Crabtree drew a derringer . . . ," *Sacramento Daily Union,* December 21, 1863; "Crabtree was evidently in liquor . . . ," *Daily Alta California,* December 20, 1863; "the most talented juvenile actress . . . ," Rourke, 185; "gives an Irish jig . . . ," "Theatrical Record," *New York Clipper,* June 11, 1864.

Chapter 6: Something New and Daring

"delighted with the original acting . . . ," *Public Ledger,* March 22, 1867; "earning both fame and fortune," *Daily Alta California,* September 25, 1865; "Might as well when you can't cover up . . . ," Comstogk; "I'm a star!" Phyllis Wynn Jackson, *Golden*

Footlights, The Merry-Making Career of Lotta Crabtree, Holiday House, NY, 1949, 253; "I had no confidence . . . ," Rourke, 246; "I'm poor Little Nell . . . ," Rourke, 199; "Lotta's face as she sits . . . ," Irene Forsyth Comer, *Little Nell and the Marchioness: Milestone in the Development of American Musical Comedy*, PhD thesis, Tufts University, Boston, 1979, 30; "sweet and tender as 'Little Nell' . . . ," "Wallack's Theatre," *Brooklyn Daily Eagle*, August 19, 1867; "I was pretty proud . . . ," Comstogk; "in 'Little Nell' she was serious . . . ," Walter Leman, *Memories of An Old Actor*, A. Roman Co., San Francisco, 1886.

Chapter 7: Tragedies and Triumphs
"turn up all right," *New Orleans Crescent*, June 4, 1868; "had not wronged her out of a penny," *Sacramento Daily Union*, June 24, 1868; "is a curious little witch . . . ," *Sacramento Daily Union*, August 20, 1869; "improved and more deserving the applause . . . ," "Amusements, Etc." *Daily Alta California*, September 11, 1869.

Chapter 8: On the Road Again
"When we go abroad . . . ," Estavan, 58; "as well as acting," Comstogk; "she never thought . . . ," Comer, 27; "hurricane of catcalls . . . ," "Life, Letters, and the Arts," *Living Age*, November 15, 1924; "the funniest thing ever done in comic dancing . . . ," Rourke, 236.

Chapter 9: Ups and Downs
"Such proceedings as stealing someone's artistic creation . . . ,"

Helena Modjeska, *Memories and Impressions of Helena Modjeska: An Autobiography*: Macmillan, New York, 1910, 376; "she is original," "Life in New York City, Lotta and Her New Play," *Brooklyn Daily Eagle*, September 21, 1884; "it seemed as if the gas were turned down," Rourke, 221; "seem like mere actors," Rourke, 221; "Lotta is a dear little soul . . . ," Alan Dale, *Queens of the Stage*, New York, 1890, 99; "Other actresses came from the stage . . . ," "Good-Bye to Lotta, Her Mother Announces a Two Years' Retirement in Europe," *New Orleans Times-Picayune*, April 11, 1883; "It will be months before I play again . . . ," *New Orleans Times-Picayune*, February 19, 1893; "My little mother is my delightful companion . . . ," *New Orleans Times-Picayune*, February 19, 1893; "an adventure," Mullenneaux, 294; "I paint," Comstogk; "Sometimes. When it does I go to the theater . . . ," Comstogk.

Chapter 10: The Golden Years
"I love to see the beautiful things flash by . . . ," Rourke, 247; "From one artiste to another . . . ," "Horse Owner Honored," *Cincinnati Enquirer*, October 12, 1907; "My secret, I think, to all success . . . ," *San Francisco Call*, July 15, 1912; "The coloring is so soft and wonderful . . . ," Laura Ingalls Wilder, *West from Home, Letters of Laura Ingalls Wilder to Almanzo Wilder, San Francisco 1915*, Harper & Row, New York, 1974, 35; "the noblest and most deserving," "Lotta and the Soldiers," *Outlook*, October 8, 1924; "Charity is what is needed . . . ," Dempsey, 186; "It is delightful to make people laugh," *New Orleans Times-Picayune*, February 19, 1893.

Glossary

Act	a performance or a part of a play
Argonaut	a Gold Rush adventurer
Audition	a test performance
Cast	a group of performers in a show
Comedienne	a female entertainer who tells jokes or performs funny acts
Encore	an additional performance demanded by an audience after the end of a show
Galop	a lively, popular nineteenth-century dance
Leprechaun	a mischievous elf in Irish tales
Lines	the words an actor or actress speaks
Lyrics	the words of a song
Melodeon	a small theater that trained people in show business
Mime	to perform with facial expressions and gestures but without words
Minstrel	a comic musician, usually a white performer in blackface
Onstage	on a stage, in the audience's view
Playbill	a poster announcing a theater event
Role	an actor's part in a play
Slow study	a performer who has trouble memorizing a role and its lines
Theater critic	one who writes about a performance or play
Tour	a trip to various cities and towns to perform
Troupe	a group of traveling entertainers
Wings	the unseen area on either side of the stage usually hidden by curtains

Bibliography

Books, Newspapers, and Articles

*Books for young readers

Bates, Helen Marie. *Lotta's Last Season.* Brattleboro, VT: privately printed, 1940.

Baur, John E. *Growing Up with California: A History of California's Children.* Los Angeles: Kramer, 1978.

Bridgeport (CT) Telegram. "Lotta Crabtree Bequeaths $4,000,000 to Charities." September 30, 1924.

Brooklyn Daily Eagle. "Life in New York City, Lotta and Her New Play." September 21, 1884.

Brooklyn Daily Eagle. "Wallack's Theatre." August 19, 1867.

Cary, Diana Serra. "The 'California Diamond,' Young Lotta Crabtree, Rose to Fame in the Rough Gold Rush Country." *Wild West* 11, no. 1, June 1998.

Chicago Inner-Ocean. "Lotta and the Newsboys." October 1, 1888.

Cincinnati Enquirer. "Horse Owner Honored." October 12, 1907.

Clappe, Louise A. (Dame Shirley). *The Shirley Letters from the California Mines, 1851-1852.* New York: Ballantine, 1949 (republished).

Coad, Oral, and Edwin Mims, Jr. *The American Stage.* New Haven: Yale University Press, 1929.

Comer, Irene Forsyth. *Little Nell and the Marchioness: Milestone in the Development of American Musical Comedy.* Ph.D. thesis, Tufts University, 1979.

Comstogk, Jarah. "A Personal Interview with Lotta." *San Francisco Call*, May 5, 1901.

Daily Alta California. "Amusements, Etc." August 18, 1869.

Daily Alta California. "Amusements, Etc." September 11, 1869.

Daily Alta California. December 20, 1863.

Daily Alta California. September 25, 1865.

Dale, Alan. *Queens of the Stage.* New York: 1890.

Dempsey, David, and Raymond Baldwin. *The Triumphs and Trials of Lotta Crabtree.* New York: William Morrow, 1968.

*Dickens, Mary Angela. *Children's Stories from Dickens.* New York: Derrydale, 1993.

Eifler, Mark A. *Gold Rush Capitalists, Greed and Growth in Sacramento.* Albuquerque: University of New Mexico Press, 2002.

Estavan, Lawrence, ed. "Monographs: Lotta Crabtree, John McCullough." Vol. 6, Abstract from WPA Project 8386. San Francisco: 1938.

*Freedman, Russell. *Children of the Wild West.* New York: Clarion, 1983.

*Holub, Joan. *What Was the Gold Rush?* New York: Grosset & Dunlap, 2013.

Jackson, Joseph. *Anybody's Gold: The Story of California's Mining Towns.* New York: Appleton-Century, 1941.

Jackson, Phyllis Wynn. *Golden Footlights: The Merry-Making Career of Lotta Crabtree.* New York: Holiday House, 1949.

Johnson, William Weber, et al., eds. *The Forty-Niners.* New York: Time-Life, 1974.

Kane Will. "Hundreds Remember 1906 Quake, Honor Survivors." *SFGate.* April 19, 2012. http://www.sfgate.com/.

Kansas City (MO) Daily Journal of Commerce. "The Actress and the Newsboys." May 16, 1874.

Koon, Helene Wickham. *How Shakespeare Won the West: Players and Performances in America's Gold Rush, 1849-1865.* Jefferson, NC: McFarland, 1989.

Leeper, David Rohrer. *Argonauts of 'Forty-Nine, Some Recollections of the Plains and the Diggins.* South Bend, IN, 1894.

Leman, Walter. *Memories of an Old Actor.* San Francisco, 1886.

Literary Digest. "An Actress Who Gives Millions to Crippled Veterans." October 18, 1924.

Living Age. "Life, Letters, and the Arts." November 15, 1924.

Loney, Glenn, ed. *Musical Theatre in America.* Papers and Proceedings of the Conference on the Musical Theater in America. Westport, CT: Greenwood Press, 1984.

Macarthy, Harry. "The Bonnie Blue Flag." New Orleans: A. E. Blackmar & Bro., 1861.

MacMinn, George R. *The Theater of the Golden Era in California.* Caldwell, ID: Caxton, 1941.

Martin, Linda, and Kerry Segrave. *Women in Comedy.* Secaucus, NJ, Citadel, 1986.

Memphis Public Ledger. March 22, 1867.

Merchant, Elizabeth L. *Girls from Dickens.* Philadelphia: Winston, 1929.

*Milstein, Janet. *Cool Characters for Kids!: 71 One-Minute Monologues.* Hanover, NH: Smith & Kraus, 2002.

Modjeska, Helena. *Memories and Impressions of Helena Modjeska: An Autobiography,* New York: Macmillan, 1910.

Mullenneaux, Nan. "Our Genius, Goodness, and Gumption: Child Actresses and National Identity in Mid-Nineteenth-Century America." *The Journal of the History of Childhood and Youth* 5, no. 2, Spring 2012.

New Orleans Crescent. June 4, 1868.

New Orleans Times-Picayune. February 19, 1893, 17.

New Orleans Times-Picayune. "Good-Bye to Lotta, Her Mother Announces a Two Years' Retirement in Europe." April 11, 1883.

New Orleans Times-Picayune. "Gotham Gossip." August 26, 1882.

New Orleans Times-Picayune. "Lotta Baseball Club." October 18, 1896.

New Orleans Times-Picayune. "Lovely Lotta, She Visits her Friends, the Newsboys, at their Home in Bank Place." January 31, 1881.

New Orleans Times-Picayune. "Personal and General Notes." November 14, 1884.

New York Clipper. "The Theatrical Record." June 11, 1864.

New York Times. "Home Gossip." February 11, 1872.

Outlook. "Lotta and the Soldiers." October 8, 1924.

Owens, Kenneth N. *Gold Rush Saints, California Mormons and the Great Rush for Riches.* Spokane: Clark, 2004.

Paul, Rodman Wilson. *Mining Frontiers of the Far West, 1848-1880.* New York: Holt, Rinehart, & Winston, 1963.

Powers, James T. *Twinkle Little Star, Sparkling Memories of Seventy Years,* New York: Putnam, 1939.

Roberts, Nancy. *The Gold Seekers: Gold, Ghosts, and Legends from Carolina to California.* Columbia: University of South Carolina Press, 1989.

Root, George F. "The Battle Cry of Freedom." Chicago: Root & Cady, 1862.

Rourke, Constance. *Troupers of the Gold Coast, or the Rise of Lotta Crabtree.* New York: Harcourt, 1928.

Sacramento Daily Union. August 20, 1869.

Sacramento Daily Union. December 21, 1863.

Sacramento Daily Union. January 14, 1867.

Sacramento Daily Union. June 24, 1868.

Sacramento Daily Union. September 23, 1868.

San Francisco Call. December 8, 1912.

San Francisco Call. January 26, 1897.

San Francisco Call. July 15, 1912.

San Francisco Call. "Theater on Kearny Street." January 26, 1897.

Schaeffer, Luther M. *Sketches of Travels in South America, Mexico, and California.* New York: 1860.

*Schanzer, Rosalyn. *Gold Fever!: Tales from the California Gold Rush.* Washington, DC: National Geographic Society, 1999.

Schreyer, Lowell H. *The Banjo Entertainers, Roots to Ragtime, a Banjo History.* Mankato, MN: Minnesota Heritage, 2007.

Semi-Weekly Wisconsin. September 16, 1868.

Smith, Dwight B., and Martin Kane. *Illustrated Guide to Lake*

Hopatcong for Season of 1898. Landing, NJ: reprint by Lake Hopatcong Historical Museum, 2002.

Sun. "Some Stage Beauties Who Have Made Fortunes." April 12, 1914.

Towse, John Ranken. *Sixty Years of the Theater: An Old Critic's Memories*. New York: Funk & Wagnalls, 1916.

Vermont Daily Transcript. June 1, 1868.

*Wilder, Laura Ingalls. *West from Home, Letters of Laura Ingalls Wilder to Almanzo Wilder, San Francisco 1915*. Harper & Row, NY, 1974.

Websites

"Battle Cry of Freedom, The," National Jukebox, Library of Congress, http://www.loc.gov/jukebox/recordings/detail/id/8684.

"Bonnie Blue Flag," Historic American Sheet Music, David N. Rubenstein Rare Book & Manuscript Library, Duke University, http://library.duke.edu/digitalcollections/hasm_conf0007/.

"Gold Rush," California State Library, http//www.library.ca.gov/goldrush.

"Gold Rush, The," American Experience, Public Broadcasting System, http://www.pbs.org/wgbh/amex/goldrush/.

"Notated Music: The Battle Cry of Freedom," Civil War Sheet Music Collection, Library of Congress, http/www.loc.gov/item/ihas.200001814/.

Society of California Pioneers, www.californiapioneers.org.

Virtual Museum of the City of San Francisco, http://www.sfmuseum.org.

Index